# 40 DAYS

## with

# Paul

Text copyright © Henry Wansbrough 2009
The author asserts the moral right
to be identified as the author of this work

Published by
The Bible Reading Fellowship
15 The Chambers, Vineyard
Abingdon OX14 3FE
United Kingdom
Tel: +44 (0)1865 319700
Email: enquiries@brf.org.uk
Website: www.brf.org.uk

ISBN 978 1 84101 685 6
First published 2009
10 9 8 7 6 5 4 3 2 1 0
All rights reserved

Acknowledgments
Scripture quotations are taken from the New Jerusalem Bible, published and
copyright © 1985 by Darton, Longman and Todd Ltd and les Editions du Cerf,
and by Doubleday, a division of Bantam Doubleday Dell Publishing Group,
Inc. Used by permission of Darton, Longman and Todd Ltd, and Doubleday, a
division of Random House, Inc.

A catalogue record for this book is available from the British Library

Printed in Great Britain by CPI Bookmarque, Croydon

# 40 DAYS
with
*Paul*

Henry Wansbrough

# Contents

# Introduction

The Year of Paul, running from the festival of Saints Peter and Paul, 29 June 2008, to the same day in 2009, is an opportunity and encouragement to read and reflect on the writings of Paul the apostle. Paul was a tireless missionary and the first Christian writer, penning his letters to the churches some years before the Gospels were written. He was a great thinker and theologian in the Jewish tradition, who saw Jesus as the Christ, the Messiah, the fulfilment of the hopes of Judaism. To Paul we owe the development of thought about God, Christ and the Christian life which stands at the beginning of the Christian tradition. By reflecting on his writings we can penetrate ever more deeply into the meaning of the Christian message and how it should shape our lives.

This little book is arranged as a series of 40 readings from Paul, and each is followed by an explanation and reflection on the text. The first four readings are intended as a brief introduction to Paul, his personality and his vision. Then follows a semi-continuous reading of the letters, principally those to the Thessalonians, the Galatians, the Romans and the Corinthians. I have also included some readings from the disputed letters to the Colossians and Ephesians, but not the so-called Pastoral Letters. This is partly for reasons of time and space, partly because most biblical scholars no longer consider the Pastorals to have been written by Paul.

For those who would like to adopt this book as their

reading for Lent 2009, the appendix offers reflections on the (Roman Catholic) lectionary readings for each of the six Sundays leading up to Easter (see pages 130–143).

# 1

# The Authority of a Servant

## 2 CORINTHIANS 11:22–30

Are they Hebrews? So am I. Are they Israelites? So am I. Are they descendants of Abraham? So am I. Are they servants of Christ? I speak in utter folly—I am too, and more than they are: I have done more work, I have been in prison more, I have been flogged more severely, many times exposed to death. Five times I have been given the thirty-nine lashes by the Jews; three times I have been beaten with sticks; once I was stoned; three times I have been shipwrecked, and once I have been in the open sea for a night and a day; continually travelling, I have been in danger from rivers, in danger from brigands, in danger from my own people and in danger from the gentiles, in danger in the towns and in danger in the open country, in danger at sea and in danger from people masquerading as brothers. I have worked with unsparing energy, for many nights without sleep; I have been hungry and thirsty, and often altogether without food or drink; I have been cold and lacked clothing. And, besides all the external things, there is, day in day out, the pressure on me of my anxiety for all the churches. If anyone weakens, I am weakened as well; and when anyone is made to fall, I burn in agony myself. If I have to boast, I will boast of all the ways in which I am weak.

Paul is writing to the Christians of Corinth, comparing himself to the 'super-apostles'. The church at Corinth was a community founded by Paul, over which he took special care. Evidently some Christian teachers had arrived in the city, claiming to be superior to Paul and more authoritative than him. Paul replies that his authority is founded on being the Servant of the Lord Jesus. Just as Jesus saw himself as the Servant of the Lord, according to the model of the Servant described by the prophet Isaiah, and particularly the Suffering Servant of Isaiah 53, so Paul sees himself as the Servant of the Lord Jesus. So he sets out to show that he has served more generously and suffered more than all these 'super-apostles'. This is the foundation of his claim to be an authentic and authoritative teacher of Christianity.

For us this passage is valuable because it gives us a picture of Paul's apostolic work. In the dozen or so years of his missionary journeys he must have travelled thousands of miles on foot, sometimes on the fine Roman roads that crisscrossed the empire (although it is likely that he would have been pushed off these when a detachment of military passed). At other times he had to find his way on tracks through the rough bush. There were no handy motels along the way, and often he must have bedded down beside the road. He outlines the danger for the solitary traveller: subject to attacks by robbers (the less kit there was to steal, the better), wild animals, village dogs and so on. The 39 lashes was a punishment imposed in the synagogues by 'my own people', perhaps for boldly expressing his attitude to the Law. The beating with sticks was a Roman punishment, perhaps for proclaiming that Christ, not the Emperor, was the Lord. One story of shipwreck comes in Acts 27, but the day and the night in the open sea must have been on another occasion.

Every line of this letter bears witness to Paul's passionate zeal to teach his young communities about the gospel and to lead them along the road to Christ, fostering them like a worried parent.

*If I have to bear hardship in witnessing to you and declaring my faith, give me, Lord, courage to do so.*

# 2

# The Lighter Side of Paul

PHILEMON 9–20

I am rather appealing to your love, being what I am, Paul, an old man, and now also a prisoner of Christ Jesus. I am appealing to you for a child of mine, whose father I became while wearing these chains: I mean Onesimus. He was of no use to you before, but now he is useful both to you and to me. I am sending him back to you—that is to say, sending you my own heart. I should have liked to keep him with me; he could have been a substitute for you, to help me while I am in the chains that the gospel has brought me. However, I did not want to do anything without your consent; it would have been forcing your act of kindness, which should be spontaneous. I suppose you have been deprived of Onesimus for a time, merely so that you could have him back for ever, no longer as a slave, but something much better than a slave, a dear brother; especially dear to me, but how much more to you, both on the natural plane and in the Lord. So if you grant me any fellowship with yourself, welcome him as you would me; if he has wronged you in any way or owes you anything, put it down to my account. I am writing this in my own hand: I, Paul, shall pay it back—I make no mention of a further debt, that you owe your very self to me! Well then, brother, I am counting on you, in the Lord; set my heart at rest, in Christ.

This little letter, or note, to Philemon gives us a chance to appreciate Paul's light-hearted wit. It is a very personal letter, full of puns and humour. And all this written from prison!

Onesimus was a slave of Philemon, and his name means 'Useful'. Paul plays with the meanings 'useful' and 'useless' throughout the letter. There are two theories about what had happened. Either Onesimus had run away to Paul from Philemon, having possibly stolen from his master too, or Philemon had lent Onesimus to Paul for a limited period, which had now expired. The former alternative is a little unlikely, since the penalty for a runaway slave was normally a gruesome death. Onesimus would have needed a lot of confidence to run away from his master and seek refuge with Paul. In any case, Onesimus had become a Christian, and so was now a 'dear brother' to Philemon. Paul sends him back to Philemon but asks Philemon to let him come again for a further period, during which he can be 'useful' to Paul.

Paul does not question the institution of slavery but the warmth and affection with which he regards Onesimus is most unusual for those times. It was rare indeed for a slave to be treated other than as an expendable chattel, whereas Paul's regard for his brother Onesimus is clear: 'I am sending you my own heart.' It would be many more centuries before it became clear that slavery was incompatible with Christianity. The full implications of the freedom and brotherhood brought by Christ would take time to mature.

It is amusing also to see how Paul attempts to twist Philemon's arm, promising to put any debt down 'to his own account', stressing his own affection for Philemon and promising to come and stay. He reminds Philemon that he is an old man and that he is in chains for the sake of the gospel. He also gently reminds him that Philemon owes his whole being to Paul, who had brought him to Christianity; for, as a Christian, Philemon—like Onesimus—is a new creation. Paul does not give Philemon much alternative!

*Lord, grant me to be light-hearted as well as serious in my total commitment to you.*

# Strength in Weakness

## 2 CORINTHIANS 12:1–10

I am boasting because I have to. Not that it does any good, but I will move on to visions and revelations from the Lord. I know a man in Christ who fourteen years ago—still in the body? I do not know; or out of the body? I do not know: God knows—was caught up right into the third heaven. And I know that this man—still in the body? or outside the body? I do not know, God knows— was caught up into Paradise and heard words said that cannot and may not be spoken by any human being. On behalf of someone like that I am willing to boast, but I am not going to boast on my own behalf except of my weaknesses; and then, if I do choose to boast I shall not be talking like a fool because I shall be speaking the truth. But I will not go on in case anybody should rate me higher than he sees and hears me to be, because of the exceptional greatness of the revelations.

Wherefore, so that I should not get above myself, I was given a thorn in the flesh, a messenger from Satan to batter me and prevent me from getting above myself. About this, I have three times pleaded with the Lord that it might leave me; but he has answered me, 'My grace is enough for you: for power is at full stretch in weakness.' It is, then, about my weaknesses that I am happiest of all to boast, so that the power of Christ may rest upon me; and that is why I am glad of weaknesses, insults, constraints, persecutions and distress for Christ's sake. For it is when I am weak that I am strong.

❦

In chapter 9 of the Acts of the Apostles, Luke tells us the story of Paul's encounter with the risen Christ on the road to Damascus. This is often called 'the conversion of Saul', but perhaps a more apt title would be 'Saul's vocation'. Did Saul really convert? He did not abandon Judaism but remained fully committed to it, and proud of his Jewishness. Rather, he came to the realization that Christ was the fulfilment of Judaism, the fulfilment of the promises made long ago to Abraham. It is an attractive idea that, while the account in Acts is an exterior account, this passage in Corinthians gives us the intimate, inner story of Paul's own experience of that event. The date of 'fourteen years ago' would fit this view. If it was not the actual event on the road to Damascus, it must have been an experience of similar significance soon afterwards. Paul is obviously talking about himself, though he delicately avoids using the first person.

Paul tells the story in terms of the world-picture of the times. Above the (flat) earth is a series of domes, the heavens. The visionary penetrates to the most sacred and intimate of these, and there has an inexpressible experience. Like any profound experience—love, fear, contentment—it cannot directly be described but only hinted at in terms of images. It was the experience of the Lord that formed Paul and supplied the motive force and inexhaustible thrust for his whole missionary endeavour.

At the same time, and no less importantly, Paul was made aware of a contrary or limiting force in himself which made him realize that he must rely not on his own efforts but on the power of Christ. He does not wish to explain to us what this was, and all attempts to guess have been fruitless. We simply do not and cannot know. More important is the fact that although Paul begged to be freed from it, he was finally glad that it made him rely on Christ's power rather than his own resources. It gave him a confidence in his mission despite all difficulties and disappointments.

*Lord, give me confidence in your strength and in the knowledge that I do not need to rely on my own ability.*

# Alive in Christ

PHILIPPIANS 1:13–24

My chains in Christ have become well known not only to all the Praetorium, but to everybody else, and so most of the brothers in the Lord have gained confidence from my chains and are getting more and more daring in announcing the Message without any fear. It is true that some of them are preaching Christ out of malice and rivalry; but there are many as well whose intentions are good; some are doing it out of love, knowing that I remain firm in my defence of the gospel. There are others who are proclaiming Christ out of jealousy, not in sincerity but meaning to add to the weight of my chains. But what does it matter? Only that in both ways, whether with false motives or true, Christ is proclaimed, and for that I am happy; and I shall go on being happy, too, because I know that this is what will save me, with your prayers and with the support of the Spirit of Jesus Christ; all in accordance with my most confident hope and trust that I shall never have to admit defeat, but with complete fearlessness I shall go on, so that now, as always, Christ will be glorified in my body, whether by my life or my death. Life to me, of course, is Christ, but then death would be a positive gain. On the other hand again, if to be alive in the body gives me an opportunity for fruitful work, I do not know which I should choose. I am caught in this dilemma: I want to be gone and to be with Christ, and this is by far the stronger desire—and yet for your sake to stay alive in this body is a more urgent need.

❮ ❯

Paul writes from prison to his beloved community at Philippi, a colony of retired soldiers in the north of Greece. They seem to have been his favourite community and he writes to them with affection and carefree openness. Only from them would he accept gifts of money, sure that these were a sign of true affection rather than a means of establishing a relationship of dependence which would demand repayment in some way.

Paul here shows the twin poles of his life: his devotion to Christ and his care for the young Christian communities he has formed. He knows that he is united with Christ in such an intimate way that he can say that his life 'is Christ', not merely 'in Christ' but wholly assimilated to Christ. His life-principle is Christ's Spirit, in ways to which he will return again and again in his writings. Nevertheless he longs for the completion of this union. He sees death not as a loss but as gain, since it completes his union to Christ.

We do not know where he was imprisoned—two possibilities are Ephesus and Caesarea—but the 'Praetorium' of which he speaks must be the Roman garrison. There would have been a significant Roman garrison at each of these places, capitols of the province of Asia and of Judea respectively. This suggests that he is conscious of the threat of martyrdom. He looks forward to it fearlessly, seeing it as the glorification of Christ in his body.

At the same time he is fully aware that his nascent Christian communities still need his help. He travelled round from one community to another and can hardly have had time to instruct them fully. The letters he writes in answer to their queries, difficulties and misunderstandings show their need for his continuing attention. He treats them as his beloved children, saying that they have many teachers but only one father, and sometimes using the image of having given birth to them. There was much that was new in Christianity, and a firm hand of guidance was essential as they progressed to a deeper understanding of its implications.

*Lord Jesus, let me not fear death, but see it as deepening my union with you.*

# Waiting for Jesus

## 1 THESSALONIANS 1:2–10

We always thank God for you all, mentioning you in our prayers continually. We remember before our God and Father how active is the faith, how unsparing the love, how persevering the hope which you have from our Lord Jesus Christ. We know, brothers loved by God, that you have been chosen, because our gospel came to you not only in words, but also in power and in the Holy Spirit and with great effect. And you observed the sort of life we lived when we were with you, which was for your sake. You took us and the Lord as your model, welcoming the word with the joy of the Holy Spirit in spite of great hardship. And so you became an example to all believers in Macedonia and Achaia since it was from you that the word of the Lord rang out—and not only throughout Macedonia and Achaia, for your faith in God has spread everywhere. We do not need to tell other people about it: other people tell us how we started the work among you, how you broke with the worship of false gods when you were converted to God and became servants of the living and true God; and how you are now waiting for Jesus, his Son, whom he raised from the dead, to come from heaven. It is he who saves us from the Retribution which is coming.

❦

1 Thessalonians is generally accepted as the first of Paul's letters, and so the very first Christian writing that we have. Paul always likes to start his letters with the conventional greeting (v. 1) and then go on to a thanksgiving for the faith of the community to which he is writing. The only exception to this, as we shall see, is the letter to the Galatians. There are two features about these thanksgivings: they are always complimentary to the recipients and they always touch on the main subject of the letter.

It is a good idea to begin with a little flattery! It puts the hearers in a good mood, especially as the letters would be read out in the worship assembly. They would be read aloud because literacy was at a low level in the Greco-Roman world—as low as seven per cent according to some estimates. In any case, multiple copies were out of the question.

In verse 8 Paul commends the Thessalonians for their faith, which had spread throughout the surrounding regions. Thessalonica was, and is, a port town, on the main Roman road system, and it is not surprising that news of their conversion and faith had spread to the other cities of Macedonia and Achaia.

At the end of the thanksgiving, Paul raises the main topic of his letter: the coming of Christ. Paul had obviously taught them that Christ had conquered death and that he was soon to come again to gather his followers to himself. 'Then they will see the Son of man coming in the clouds with great power and glory,' says Jesus in the Gospel of Mark (13:26). Presumably members of the

Christian community at Thessalonica had died and their families and friends were concerned that the dead would miss out on the coming of Christ. Had Paul deceived them, or got it wrong? The early Christians' expectation of the triumphant coming of Christ was so vivid that they were eagerly awaiting it. After all, Jesus had said, 'The kingdom of God has come near' or 'has come upon you' (Luke 10:9, 11). One of their watchwords, retained in Aramaic even in these Greek letters, was 'Maranatha', which may be translated either 'Come, Lord!' or 'Our Lord is coming'.

*Whenever I am to meet you, Lord, let me be eager and ready.*

# Like a Mother

1 THESSALONIANS 2:7b–14

Like a mother feeding and looking after her children, we felt so devoted to you, that we would have been happy to share with you not only the gospel of God, but also our own lives, so dear had you become. You remember, brothers, with what unsparing energy we used to work, slaving night and day so as not to be a burden on any one of you while we were proclaiming the gospel of God to you. You are witnesses, and so is God, that our treatment of you, since you believed, has been impeccably fair and upright. As you know, we treated every one of you as a father treats his children, urging you, encouraging you and appealing to you to live a life worthy of God, who calls you into his kingdom and his glory.

Another reason why we continually thank God for you is that as soon as you heard the word that we brought you as God's message, you welcomed it for what it really is, not the word of any human being, but God's word, a power that is working among you believers. For you, my brothers, have modelled yourselves on the churches of God in Christ Jesus which are in Judaea, in that you have suffered the same treatment from your own countrymen as they have had from the Jews.

There could never be any doubt about Paul's devotion to the communities he founded; we have already seen the hardships he endured for them in his apostolic travels. He often uses the language of parenting, referring to himself as both father and mother. 'Even though you might have ten thousand slaves to look after you in Christ, you still have no more than one father, and it was I who fathered you in Christ Jesus', he writes to the Corinthians (1 Corinthians 4:15).

Paul also protests that he was 'slaving night and day so as not to be a burden on any one of you' (v. 9). This points to a tricky financial situation: even today 'there's no such thing as a free lunch'. In the ancient world, even more than today, to accept money from someone implied acceptance of an inferior status and a permanent obligation to support the donor. According to Acts, Paul worked as a tent-maker. This not only meant that he could be self-supporting, it also meant that he did not have to carry much kit on his travels—for tents were made of skins, and he would need only needle and thread and a knife for preparing the skins.

Paul was always aware that Jerusalem was the mother church and model for the other Christian communities. He was careful to check that his apostolate was acceptable to the 'pillars' of the church (Galatians 2:2). Although there would later be difficulties between the Jerusalem church and Paul about observance of the Jewish Law, he still determined to heal the breach by making a collection of money for the poor in Jerusalem.

Paul says that the Thessalonians modelled themselves on the churches of Judea. The Jewish communities scattered round the Roman world were normally ruled by a body of elders with a temporary president, and Acts 14:23 says that Paul set up elders in his first communities. However, it is only when writing to the Philippians that he greets the 'presiding elders and the deacons' (Philippians 1:1). There were certainly no such officials at Corinth.

*Lord, give to your Church worthy leaders, endowed with the zeal, care and devotion of Paul.*

# 7

# The Day of the Lord

1 THESSALONIANS 4:13—5:4

We want you to be quite certain, brothers, about those who have fallen asleep, to make sure that you do not grieve for them, as others do who have no hope. We believe that Jesus died and rose again, and that in the same way God will bring with him those who have fallen asleep in Jesus. We can tell you this from the Lord's own teaching, that we who are still alive for the Lord's coming will not have any advantage over those who have fallen asleep. At the signal given by the voice of the Archangel and the trumpet of God, the Lord himself will come down from heaven; those who have died in Christ will be the first to rise, and only after that shall we who remain alive be taken up in the clouds, together with them, to meet the Lord in the air. This is the way we shall be with the Lord for ever. With such thoughts as these, then, you should encourage one another.

About times and dates, brothers, there is no need to write to you for you are well aware in any case that the Day of the Lord is going to come like a thief in the night. It is when people are saying, 'How quiet and peaceful it is' that sudden destruction falls on them, as suddenly as labour pains come on a pregnant woman; and there is no escape. But you, brothers, do not live in the dark, that the Day should take you unawares like a thief.

❦

Now Paul begins to answer directly the worried question of his correspondents. He uses the imagery of the Roman triumphal procession. After a great victory, a Roman general (normally the Emperor) would conduct a grand triumphal procession to the capital in Rome, leading his victorious troops, and with the captives in chains. Now it is Jesus, not the Emperor, who leads the triumph, and on the clouds! There is no need to worry, says Paul: far from missing out, Christians who have already died will take precedence over those who are still alive.

This picture of Jesus as a triumphant Emperor is, of course, only imagery. We do not need to believe that this will occur literally, any more than that there will be a literal last judgment with sheep and goats (as in Matthew 25). Incidentally, it is notable that Paul is so focused on the triumph of Christ and his followers that he does not, either here or elsewhere, even consider the fate of 'goats'.

The major difficulty for us is that Paul thinks that this event will happen fairly soon. Was he wrong? Is he giving false teaching? What did Jesus think and teach? Some scholars think that Jesus expected the world to end at his death. For Christians it is certainly true that the world, as it was, came to an end with the death and resurrection of Jesus. Everything was changed. Paul occasionally uses the language of a 'new creation'. For us, the world was utterly changed with the triumph of Christ. This does not mean that Jesus expected the space/time continuum of the universe to be shattered. He was using the dramatic imagery of the biblical Day of the Lord, when God would set everything right on earth, punishing the wicked and rewarding the just. This had always been pictured in earth-shattering terms of cosmic disturbances, stars falling from heaven and so on. It was indeed to be a reversal, but not in the material terms portrayed in that imagery. The New Testament teaches that it is imminent, in the sense that we must take action now. It teaches nothing about the timing of the event.

*Lord Jesus, help me to prepare now for your coming, whenever that may be.*

# 8

# Preparing for Judgment

2 THESSALONIANS 2:2–10

Please do not be too easily thrown into confusion or alarmed by any manifestation of the Spirit or any statement or any letter claiming to come from us, suggesting that the Day of the Lord has already arrived. Never let anyone deceive you in any way. It cannot happen until the Great Revolt has taken place and there has appeared the wicked One, the lost One, the Enemy, who raises himself above every so-called God or object of worship to enthrone himself in God's sanctuary and flaunts the claim that he is God. Surely you remember my telling you about this when I was with you? And you know, too, what is still holding him back from appearing before his appointed time. The mystery of wickedness is already at work, but let him who is restraining it once be removed, and the wicked One will appear openly. The Lord will destroy him with the breath of his mouth and will annihilate him with his glorious appearance at his coming.

But the coming of the wicked One will be marked by Satan being at work in all kinds of counterfeit miracles and signs and wonders, and every wicked deception aimed at those who are on the way to destruction because they would not accept the love of the truth and so be saved.

Paul's first letter must have thrown the Thessalonians into a panic, as they appear to have imagined that the Lord's triumphant procession was going to occur at any moment. So Paul writes again to calm them: a lot of water must flow under the bridge before all this happens, and he details some of the events that must occur before the end. Over the centuries, both prophets of doom and campaigners against various movements have seen 'the Great Revolt' and 'the Enemy' to be exemplified in various historical figures and movements, usually their own particular enemies or bugbears. These too, however, are images that are not intended to be cashed into any particular event or person.

Paul is again using scriptural imagery, originally used by the prophet Ezekiel (28:2), referring to the proud king of Tyre, who thought to exalt himself as a god and was to come crashing to his doom. Such 'apocalyptic' language was commonly used in first-century Jewish writing. Such features as strange semi-human figures appearing, passing from earth to heaven and back, and the use of lurid imagery and symbolic numbers, are common. In the Bible the most extensive use of them comes in the Revelation (or 'Apocalypse') of John, the final book of the New Testament. They do, however, occur also elsewhere, for example in the account of the transfiguration in the Gospels.

The message is that we are now, each of us, in the time of trial or testing. We need not expect any literal cataclysmic series of events to precede the end. It is not even necessary to believe that there will be a single judgment scene for us all simultaneously, as Matthew's scene of the last judgment depicts—for this, too, is apocalyptic language. The Church teaches that each of us is to be judged individually at death when we meet the Lord, and it is this judgment that we need to prepare for now.

*Lead us not into temptation, but deliver us from the Evil One.*

# 9

# Justified by Faith

PHILIPPIANS 3:3–14

We are the true people of the circumcision since we worship by the Spirit of God and make Christ Jesus our only boast, not relying on physical qualifications, although I myself could rely on these too. If anyone does claim to rely on them, my claim is better. Circumcised on the eighth day of my life, I was born of the race of Israel, of the tribe of Benjamin, a Hebrew born of Hebrew parents. In the matter of the Law, I was a Pharisee; as for religious fervour, I was a persecutor of the Church; as for the uprightness embodied in the Law, I was faultless. But what were once my assets I now through Christ Jesus count as losses. Yes, I will go further: because of the supreme advantage of knowing Christ Jesus my Lord, I count everything else as loss. For him I have accepted the loss of all other things, and look on them all as filth if only I can gain Christ and be given a place in him, with the uprightness I have gained not from the Law, but through faith in Christ, an uprightness from God, based on faith, that I may come to know him and the power of his resurrection, and partake of his sufferings by being moulded to the pattern of his death, striving towards the goal of resurrection from the dead. Not that I have secured it already, nor yet reached my goal, but I am still pursuing it in the attempt to take hold of the prize for which Christ Jesus took hold of me. Brothers, I do not reckon myself as having taken hold of it; I can only say that forgetting all that lies behind me, and straining forward to what lies in front, I am racing towards the finishing-point to win the prize of God's heavenly call in Christ Jesus.

❧ ❧

Whatever Paul may say about devaluing everything but Christ, it is clear that on the human level he is still quite proud of titles of nobility in Judaism. Paul is a Jew through and through. According to Acts 22:3, he claims that he was trained by Gamaliel, the most famous Jerusalem rabbi of that generation. He knows his scripture thoroughly; he respects the figures of Jewish history; he uses Jewish methods of argument, often skilfully turning them upside down so that they argue for Christianity. It is all the more striking that, by comparison with the advantages of Christianity, these titles are nothing.

Most importantly, Paul contrasts uprightness won by the Jewish Law with uprightness won by faith. This will form a central argument, as we shall see, in Romans. At first sight Paul's position is quite paradoxical, since the Greek word for 'uprightness' is a word obviously related to 'law'. It could also be translated 'justness' or 'justification', and justness is closely related to conformity to the demands of law. So it would seem obvious that uprightness/justification/justness should at least be related to legal observance. Yet Paul says that it has nothing to do with legal observance, but only with faith, by which he means hanging on by one's fingertips to the promises of God and trusting in them. It is unclear whether most Jews thought that justification could positively be earned through the works of the Law, or whether observance of the Law was simply regarded as a criterion of belonging to Israel, a 'boundary marker' to show who qualified and who did not qualify for the salvation promised to Abraham and his descendants.

Besides Paul's skill in Jewish and rabbinic argument, he is equally skilled in Greek rhetoric. In this passage we can see his neat and amusing use of the financial images of profit and loss (v. 7). He takes another set of images from the games: here it is the image of running a race to win a prize (v. 12). Metaphors of sport, running and boxing are often found in Paul. They seem especially apt when we remember that he is writing to a Roman colony of retired soldiers at Philippi.

*Lord, you have won our righteousness for us, and it is only through you that we can receive it.*

# 10

# Permeated with Christ

PHILIPPIANS 4:4–15a

Always be joyful, then, in the Lord; I repeat, be joyful. Let your good sense be obvious to everybody. The Lord is near. Never worry about anything; but tell God all your desires of every kind in prayer and petition shot through with gratitude, and the peace of God which is beyond our understanding will guard your hearts and your thoughts in Christ Jesus. Finally, brothers, let your minds be filled with everything that is true, everything that is honourable, everything that is upright and pure, everything that we love and admire—with whatever is good and praiseworthy. Keep doing everything you learnt from me and were told by me and have heard or seen me doing. Then the God of peace will be with you.

As for me, I am full of joy in the Lord, now that at last your consideration for me has blossomed again; though I recognize that you really did have consideration before, but had no opportunity to show it. I do not say this because I have lacked anything; I have learnt to manage with whatever I have. I know how to live modestly, and I know how to live luxuriously too: in every way now I have mastered the secret of all conditions: full stomach and empty stomach, plenty and poverty. There is nothing I cannot do in the One who strengthens me. All the same, it was good of you to share with me in my hardships. In the early days of the gospel, as you of Philippi well know, when I left Macedonia, no church other than yourselves made common account with me in the matter of expenditure and receipts.

❮ ❯

This outbreak of joy makes a suitable final paragraph of the letter. In fact, there are two separate outbreaks of joy, which has led some to wonder whether the letter as we now know it was originally a collection of several letters. If so, one of these would have ended suitably at verse 9, with 'the God of peace will be with you', making the final dozen verses of the epistle a separate letter, thanking the Philippians for their gifts of money. On the other hand, it is equally possible to see these final verses as an impetuous afterthought or postscript by Paul to the same letter. Either way, Paul's words on joy, tranquillity and peace in the Lord are inspiring.

Here again, as so often, it is Paul's awareness of living in the life of the risen Lord that inspires him and fills him with joy and confidence. It gives him the sense that there is nothing he cannot do and nothing he cannot endure. This is a recurrent theme in the letters, colouring Paul's whole approach to life. On what is it founded, and what does it amount to? He has already expressed at the opening of the letter this same joy and confidence under threat of death (1:18–23). Paul's experience on the road to Damascus, as recounted in Acts 9:4–6 and elsewhere, is the basis on which Paul thought that in persecuting Christians he had been trying to persecute Christ himself.

At the same time, in Galatians 3:1–3 Paul appeals to the tangible experience of the power of the Lord working among Christians, to convince them that the Spirit of Christ is really alive in them. The same argument is expressed in the list of works of the Spirit later in the same letter (5:22–23) and in the description of the powerful activity of Christ's Spirit in the Corinthian community (despite all its faults) in 1 Corinthians 12 to 14. In Romans 6, Paul's joy and confidence are related to the experience of being 'dipped' into Christ at baptism. Acceptance of baptism expresses the idea of putting all one's hope and trust in Christ. The Christian is then 'dipped' into Christ's death and so is permeated with Christ, or soaked in Christ and Christ's risen life.

*'Give me joy in my heart, keep me praising. Keep me praising till the break of day.'*

# 11

# A Sharp Rebuke

GALATIANS 1:1–10

From Paul, an apostle appointed not by human beings nor through any human being but by Jesus Christ and God the Father who raised him from the dead, and all the brothers who are with me, to the churches of Galatia. Grace and peace from God the Father and our Lord Jesus Christ who gave himself for our sins to liberate us from this present wicked world, in accordance with the will of our God and Father, to whom be glory for ever and ever. Amen.

I am astonished that you are so promptly turning away from the one who called you in the grace of Christ and are going over to a different gospel—not that it is another gospel; except that there are trouble-makers among you who are seeking to pervert the gospel of Christ. But even if we ourselves or an angel from heaven preaches to you a gospel other than the one we preached to you, let God's curse be on him. I repeat again what we declared before: anyone who preaches to you a gospel other than the one you were first given is to be under God's curse. Whom am I trying to convince now, human beings or God? Am I trying to please human beings? If I were still doing that I should not be a servant of Christ.

Contrary to his usual style of a greeting followed by thanksgiving for the faith and achievements of his correspondents, Paul weighs into his subject immediately. He is disappointed and furious with the Christians of Galatia. So he first stresses his authority as an apostle, appointed as such not by any human being but by Jesus Christ himself (v. 1)—which means that no human being has any right to contradict him. Then, instead of the usual courteous 'I give thanks…' comes the curt 'I am astonished…'. What has been going on?

Paul had brought the good news of Jesus the Christ—that is, the Messiah of Judaism—to Jewish communities in Galatia and they had responded by willingly accepting him. Then some representatives of the church at Jerusalem had come along and told them that they must still obey the Jewish Law. This was totally alien to Paul's message that salvation is won by putting complete trust in Christ and his resurrection. In his rebuke Paul is brutally frank with these converts of his, stressing his personal authority and the total reversal that the move to Christianity involved in his own way of life. He likens himself to the prophet Jeremiah, who was also called 'from his mother's womb' (v. 15; Jeremiah 1:5) to speak the hard truth to his contemporaries. Then he goes on to recount the support for his stance that he had received from the Jerusalem church and from Peter himself. Incidentally, this gives us a valuable insight into Paul's life and the interrelationship of the leaders of the

Church, about which we would otherwise have known nothing.

It was obviously a new and puzzling situation. Paul had taught that Jesus was the completion of all the hopes of Judaism. The practice of the Law was now utterly irrelevant. But how could the fulfilment of Judaism imply departure from the whole Jewish way of life dictated by the Law? So argued those whom Paul considers 'trouble-makers', but when a new situation arises there are bound to be many who want to stay as close as possible to the old ways.

*Lord, grant me discernment when I face difficult decisions and guide my ways according to your will.*

# 12

# Divided Loyalties

GALATIANS 2:7–14

Once they saw that the gospel for the uncircumcised had
been entrusted to me, just as to Peter the gospel for the
circumcised (for he who empowered Peter's apostolate
to the circumcision also empowered mine to the gentiles), and when they acknowledged the grace that had
been given to me, then James and Cephas and John, who
were the ones recognized as pillars, offered their right
hands to Barnabas and to me as a sign of partnership: we
were to go to the gentiles and they to the circumcised.
They asked nothing more than that we should remember
to help the poor, as indeed I was anxious to do in any
case.

However, when Cephas came to Antioch, then I did
oppose him to his face since he was manifestly in the
wrong. Before certain people from James came, he
used to eat with gentiles; but as soon as these came, he
backed out and kept apart from them, out of fear of the
circumcised. And the rest of the Jews put on the same
act as he did, so that even Barnabas was carried away
by their insincerity.

When I saw, though, that their behaviour was not true
to the gospel, I said to Cephas in front of all of them,
'Since you, though you are a Jew, live like the gentiles

and not like the Jews, how can you compel the gentiles to live like the Jews?'

❦

Paul is insisting to the Galatians that no church authority ever laid down that Christians of Jewish origin need continue to obey the Jewish Law. He had explained to the authorities at Jerusalem how he understood the situation, and they had not demanded that Titus, a Gentile Christian, be circumcised. That is, of course, a slightly different case: if a Gentile Christian need not obey the Law, it does not necessarily follow that a Christian of Jewish origin is free of its obligations. In any case, however, Paul is arguing that obedience to the prescriptions of the Law is irrelevant to salvation. He now goes on to explain that the leaders of the Church had set out different spheres of activity for himself and Cephas. (Cephas is the Aramaic name for Peter; both words mean 'rock'.)

Real trouble surfaced for the first time at Antioch. Antioch was a large Jewish centre, an important port town, with a venerable Jewish colony located in the most salubrious quarter of the city. One archaeologist has described it as the 'Beverley Hills of Antioch'. It was at Antioch that the followers of Christ were first dubbed 'Christians', or 'Messianists' (Acts 11:26). It was also there that Barnabas and Paul were appointed missionaries (13:2).

Peter was at Antioch, peaceably sharing meals—and, no doubt, eucharistic meals—with Gentile Christians when delegates from the church at Jerusalem objected, presumably because they considered the Gentile Christians unclean. Peter then followed their advice and separated himself. At this Paul publicly rebuked Peter for inconsistency. It escalated into a major disagreement. Paul does not say that Peter climbed down, although it would have clinched his argument had he done so, and there is no sign that any compromise was reached. On the contrary, the two Jews, Barnabas and John Mark, split off from Paul's missionary efforts and left him to form his own team, all of whom have Greek names. It was only some years later that Paul set about healing the breach by his collection for the poor of Jerusalem among the Gentile churches. This would show due submission and gratitude to the mother church for the gift of faith.

*Lord, we pray that your Church may be one, and that its divisions may be overcome.*

# 13

# Favours of the Spirit

## GALATIANS 3:1–5

You stupid people in Galatia! After you have had a clear picture of Jesus Christ crucified, right in front of your eyes, who has put a spell on you? There is only one thing I should like you to tell me: How was it that you received the Spirit—was it by the practice of the Law, or by believing in the message you heard? Having begun in the Spirit, can you be so stupid as to end in the flesh? Can all the favours you have received have had no effect at all—if there really has been no effect? Would you say, then, that he who so lavishly sends the Spirit to you, and causes the miracles among you, is doing this through your practice of the Law or because you believed the message you heard?

❦

After his little history lesson Paul addresses the Galatians directly—and fiercely. It is the only time he calls people 'stupid', and this was to be read out publicly in the assembly of the church. This was no gentle rebuke! For us, however, the passage is invaluable.

Paul appeals to the works of the Spirit active among the Galatians. How can they explain the fact that the Spirit is at work? The Spirit did not come to them from the Law, so it must be a result of their faith in Christ. That should show them the irrelevance of the Law, its lack of power compared to Christ's. This argument presupposes that there were indeed works of the Spirit among them, to which he could appeal as tangible evidence, needing to be explained. What does he mean by the 'favours' of the Spirit? Later in the letter (5:22–23) he will give a list of 'the fruit of the Spirit'. Writing to the Corinthians, he presents a picture of the varied activities of the Spirit-led and Spirit-filled church (1 Corinthians 12 to 14). They are all activities that contribute to building up the Christian community. They need not be extraordinary 'charismatic' activities, such as speaking in tongues and miraculous healings. In fact, Paul rather plays down the gift of speaking in tongues. Ordinary Christian activities are extraordi-nary enough, such as the healing touch or the healing word to those in need or upset, and the caring activities of the Christian—whether it be motherhood, caring for the young and bringing up children in Christian ways, or providing gentle counsel that may enable the downhearted to regain their confidence. All these need the generosity, tact and sensitivity that the Spirit gives.

Another of the works of the Spirit, which Paul does not list in the letter to the Corinthians, features later in Galatians 4:6. This is prayer, the knowledge that as adopted children of God we can pray 'Abba, Father', aware that we are living by Christ's Spirit dwelling within us, and can take Jesus' prayer on our lips.

*Father, let me live by Christ's Spirit within me, with the generosity, tact and sensitivity that he gives.*

# 14

# The Blessing of Faith

GALATIANS 3:6–14

Abraham, you remember, put his faith in God, and this was reckoned to him as uprightness. Be sure, then, that it is people of faith who are the children of Abraham. And it was because scripture foresaw that God would give saving justice to the gentiles through faith, that it announced the future gospel to Abraham in the words: All nations will be blessed in you. So it is people of faith who receive the same blessing as Abraham, the man of faith.

On the other hand, all those who depend on the works of the Law are under a curse, since scripture says: Accursed be he who does not make what is written in the book of the Law effective, by putting it into practice. Now it is obvious that nobody is reckoned as upright in God's sight by the Law, since the upright will live through faith; and the Law is based not on faith but on the principle, whoever complies with it will find life in it. Christ redeemed us from the curse of the Law by being cursed for our sake since scripture says: Anyone hanged is accursed, so that the blessing of Abraham might come to the gentiles in Christ Jesus, and so that we might receive the promised Spirit through faith.

Paul here brings out a scriptural text that is basic to his idea of salvation, Genesis 15:6: 'Abraham put his faith in God and this was reckoned to him as uprightness.' He will meditate on this at length in chapter 4 of Romans, a letter that expands and develops many of the themes of Galatians. If salvation comes from faith after the model of Abraham, there is no need to pin our hopes on observance of the Law, which came 430 years later (Galatians 3:17). Abraham's faith was simply trust in God's promise when God appeared to him, bade him leave behind all his natural security and promised him protection and countless descendants. For Paul's argument it is important that this promise included the Gentiles: 'all nations on earth will bless themselves by you' (Genesis 12:3). From the beginning the Gentiles were included in the promise made to Abraham.

But what is this about Christ becoming accursed for our sake? Elsewhere Paul has also been translated as saying that Christ became 'sin' for our sake (2 Corinthians 5:21, for example NRSV). This is surely a mistake, for the same word in Hebrew means 'sin-offering', which makes much more sense. Christ could indeed be considered as becoming a sin-offering. However, the explanation of our current passage in Galatians 3:10–13 is more complicated, though interesting and valuable for the understanding of Paul. He is using the Jewish technique of interpretation called *gezerah shawah*, well-known among the rabbis. It consists of linking two or more separate passages of scripture that use the same word—in this case, 'accursed' in Deuteronomy 27:26 and 21:23, both of which he quotes here. To us it appears little more than a verbal game, but to Paul's expertly attuned mind it was a valid method of arguing. Crucifixion is elsewhere called 'hanging on a tree' (see Acts 5:30; 10:39), which enables Paul to argue that Christ put himself in the position of those who fail to obey the Law, and yet fulfilled all the demands of the Law. By thus putting himself in the position of sinful humanity, and in that position ('hanged on a tree') fulfilling the Law, Christ made the demands of the Law henceforth superfluous and irrelevant.

*We worship you, Christ, and we bless you, because by your cross you have redeemed the world.*

# 15

# Sons of God

GALATIANS 4:1–11

What I am saying is this: an heir, during the time while he is still under age, is no different from a slave, even though he is the owner of all the property; he is under the control of guardians and administrators until the time fixed by his father. So too with us, as long as we were still under age, we were enslaved to the elemental principles of this world; but when the completion of the time came, God sent his Son, born of a woman, born a subject of the Law, to redeem the subjects of the Law, so that we could receive adoption as sons. As you are sons, God has sent into our hearts the Spirit of his Son crying, 'Abba, Father'; and so you are no longer a slave, but a son; and if a son, then an heir, by God's own act.

But formerly when you did not know God, you were kept in slavery to things which are not really gods at all, whereas now that you have come to recognize God— or rather, be recognized by God—how can you now turn back again to those powerless and bankrupt elements whose slaves you now want to be all over again? You are keeping special days, and months, and seasons and years—I am beginning to be afraid that I may, after all, have wasted my efforts on you.

Paul is continuing his contrast between the restrictions of Judaism and the liberty of Christians, somewhat narrowly presenting the 'childhood' state of Judaism as a form of slavery. He is making two points at once: firstly, that Judaism is a slavery compared to the freedom of Christianity; and secondly, that Judaism makes sense only in view of its completion in Christianity, just as childhood makes sense only as a stage on the way to adulthood. This enables him to suggest that Judaism is only a passing phase, which the Galatians should have outgrown.

It is difficult to see what Paul means by speaking of Judaism as in slavery to the 'elemental principles of this world' (v. 3). The final sentence of this reading shows that he is thinking of the special obligations imposed by 'days and months and seasons and years', which are dictated by earthly and astral conditions. But these are only a minor part of Jewish religious observance. Perhaps he is objecting to being ruled by any automatic or subhuman influence.

The idea of childhood leads on to the much more positive teaching on adoption as sons as an image of the loving relationship of obedience to God. 'Abba' is the Aramaic word used by Jesus for God, his Father. It is enshrined in the prayer of the agony in the garden and in the Lord's Prayer. Perhaps the relationship is most fully described in John 5:19–31. The word was retained in Aramaic even among Greek-speaking Christians as a sort of talisman, a link to Jesus' own relationship to his

Father. It has been incorrectly considered as the loving cry of a child to a father, like 'Daddy'. In fact, it is a more adult word, expressing the warm, loving and respectful relationship of a grown son and heir to his father. Despite the need for inclusive thought and language, the concept of adoption to 'sonship' must be retained, since it includes inheritance as co-heirs with Christ. In Judaism only a son could inherit, which means that all Christians, both men and women, are adopted to sonship, not merely to the status of children of God.

*Abba, Father, not my will but yours be done.*

# 16

# Spiritual Fruit

GALATIANS 5:16–26

Instead, I tell you, be guided by the Spirit, and you will no longer yield to self-indulgence. The desires of self-indulgence are always in opposition to the Spirit, and the desires of the Spirit are in opposition to self-indulgence: they are opposites, one against the other; that is how you are prevented from doing the things that you want to. But when you are led by the Spirit, you are not under the Law. When self-indulgence is at work the results are obvious: sexual vice, impurity, and sensuality, the worship of false gods and sorcery; antagonisms and rivalry, jealousy, bad temper and quarrels, disagreements, factions and malice, drunkenness, orgies and all such things. And about these, I tell you now as I have told you in the past, that people who behave in these ways will not inherit the kingdom of God. On the other hand the fruit of the Spirit is love, joy, peace, patience, kindness, goodness, trustfulness, gentleness and self-control; no law can touch such things as these. All who belong to Christ Jesus have crucified self with all its passions and its desires.

Since we are living by the Spirit, let our behaviour be guided by the Spirit and let us not be conceited or provocative and envious of one another.

The consequences of living by the Spirit or by self-indulgence are now set out, making for a useful check-list for discerning one's principal motivations. The list concerns mostly human relationships in love and respect for others. Lists of virtues and vices were common in the ethical teaching of the time and Paul's list has many overlaps with the lists proposed by ethical teachers of that—or any—age.

'Self-indulgence' (or sometimes 'natural desires') is the translation given to the Greek word that basically means 'flesh'. It is important that behaviour contrasted with the behaviour inspired by the Spirit should not be seen as confined to the 'flesh' in the sense of 'body', as though the only vices were those led by sexual gratification or physical greed for food or drink or bodily comforts. The 'desires of the flesh' include more sophisticated drives, which might be regarded as primarily psychological, such as rivalry and malice. The 'flesh' therefore must be seen primarily as human nature, prone to failure and self-centredness, or as ordinary human behaviour not elevated by the Spirit of God.

Paul's moral teaching does not consist in precepts and rules. There are occasions when he does lay down such rules, as in the dress of women who speak in the assembly (1 Corinthians 11:5). But more often he lays down the principles of behaviour, leaving individual Christians to draw their own detailed conclusions in the light of their conscience (1 Corinthians 7—8). He assumes the motivation and guidance of the Spirit of Christ dwelling within Christians and directing all their actions. His teaching is more expansive than restrictive, encouraging an inspired liberty of action rather than a childish slavery to precepts. He assumes that, as adopted sons of God, Christians will be able to make their own judgments under the inspiration of the Spirit. Only very occasionally does he stamp his foot and uncompromisingly lay down the law (11:16). It is amusing to note that the behaviour he demands here is dictated more by social custom than by any Christian principle. When decisions involve the Christian conscience, he is much more flexible (8:12–13).

*Grant me the care and discernment, Lord, of an informed conscience, and the courage to follow it.*

# 17

# Jesus is Lord

## ROMANS 1:1–15

From Paul, a servant of Christ Jesus, called to be an apostle, set apart for the service of the gospel that God promised long ago through his prophets in the holy scriptures.

This is the gospel concerning his Son who, in terms of human nature, was born a descendant of David and who, in terms of the Spirit and of holiness, was designated Son of God in power by resurrection from the dead: Jesus Christ, our Lord, through whom we have received grace and our apostolic mission of winning the obedience of faith among all the nations for the honour of his name. You are among these, and by his call you belong to Jesus Christ. To you all, God's beloved in Rome, called to be his holy people. Grace and peace from God our Father and the Lord Jesus Christ.

First I give thanks to my God through Jesus Christ for all of you because your faith is talked of all over the world. God, whom I serve with my spirit in preaching the gospel of his Son, is my witness that I continually mention you in my prayers, asking always that by some means I may at long last be enabled to visit you, if it is God's will. For I am longing to see you so that I can convey to you some spiritual gift that will be a lasting strength, or rather that we may be strengthened together through our mutual faith, yours and mine. I want you to be quite certain too, brothers, that I have often planned to visit you—though up to the present I have always been prevented—in the hope that I might work as fruitfully among you as I have among the gentiles elsewhere. I have an obligation to Greeks as well as barbarians, to the educated as well as the ignorant, and hence the eagerness on my part to preach the gospel to you in Rome too.

⤶ ⤷

Paul's letter to the Romans is always printed at the head of the collection of his letters. This may suggest that it was the first to be written. It was not! Or perhaps it suggests that it is the greatest of his letters. Perhaps it was. In fact, the order of the letters is simply descending order of length, from the longest to the shortest, in two series: first the letters to communities, then the letters to individuals.

Rome was the capital of the empire, and Paul writes to the Christian community with obvious deference, hardly daring to offer them advice and stressing how much he looks forward to visiting them. It was a community composed of Christians sprung from both Judaism and paganism. They had been through various troubles and Paul sets out to show that each tradition needs the other, that each contributes something special to the other. He also needs their help as a line of communication for his projected mission to Spain in the far west. In Spain, Latin would be spoken, which Paul may not have understood. In addition, the Romans would have known that he had been teaching that Christians need not obey the Jewish Law. He may have felt the need to re-establish his reputation in Judaism by showing how he valued Jewish law and tradition.

As always, his opening thanksgiving hints at the matter of the letter. Jesus is 'son of David', so sprung from the Jewish tradition, but is also constituted Son of God in power by the resurrection. This brings the salvation, promised long ago through Abraham and the prophets, to 'all of you', both Jew and Gentile. This will be the programme of his letter—how salvation is brought to all through Jesus Christ and his resurrection.

Hovering underneath many of Paul's statements is the assertion that Jesus, not the Roman emperor, is Lord—the real source of power and authority and the true object of devotion. Worship of the emperor as a god was at the centre of loyalty to the Roman empire, and Paul needs to stress that for Christians the true 'Lord' can only be the Lord Jesus.

*Lord Jesus, may we see you, not any other power or authority, as the Lord.*

# 18

# God's Saving Justice

ROMANS 3:20–26

So then, no human being can be found upright at the tribunal of God by keeping the Law; all that the Law does is to tell us what is sinful.

God's saving justice was witnessed by the Law and the Prophets, but now it has been revealed altogether apart from law: God's saving justice given through faith in Jesus Christ to all who believe. No distinction is made: all have sinned and lack God's glory, and all are justified by the free gift of his grace through being set free in Christ Jesus. God appointed him as a sacrifice for reconciliation, through faith, by the shedding of his blood, and so showed his justness; first for the past, when sins went unpunished because he held his hand; and now again for the present age, to show how he is just and justifies everyone who has faith in Jesus.

So far in the letter, Paul has stressed what a mess the world is in, full of vice and corruption among both Gentiles and Jews. What is the solution? The saving justice of God. God's justice is not a punishing justice, penalizing people for not adhering to the Law. It is a justice that saves, because it is God's own justness—that is, his everlasting fidelity to the promises he made to Abraham, promises that in him Abraham would find salvation and that in Abraham all nations would be blessed. God's justice consists in the fulfilment of this promise, and human justice consists not in observance of any law, not even the Jewish Law, but simply in faith—that is, putting our trust uniquely in those promises. It does not consist in anything we do, but only in trust, in hanging on by our fingertips to God's own saving justice.

What, then, of Jesus Christ? To begin with, Paul gives a cultic explanation: Christ is presented as the *hilasterion*, the 'sacrifice of reconciliation' or the 'mercy-seat'. The word carries both meanings. It alludes to the annual Jewish Day of Reconciliation, described in Leviticus 16. There each year, after the scapegoat had ritually carried off the sins of Israel into the desert, the high priest sacrificed a bull and scattered the blood of the bull over the mercy-seat on the top of the ark of the covenant, revered as the dwelling place of God, and over the people. Blood is the symbol of life. It belongs to God alone, and the Israelites were not permitted to consume blood. This sprinkled blood brought the people new life and united them again to God.

Paul sees the sacrifice of reconciliation to be fulfilled in Christ. This is the true value of the blood of Christ. Christ is both the sacrifice of reconciliation and the mercy-seat where God and humanity meet and where the reconciliation occurs. So God's saving justice has nothing to do with obedience to the Law and comes not to those who obey the Law but to those who put their trust in Jesus.

*Give me true life in the blood of Christ, that I may be reconciled to the Father in faith and trust.*

# 19

# Christ's Obedience

## ROMANS 5:12–21

Well then; it was through one man that sin came into the world, and through sin death, and thus death has spread through the whole human race because everyone has sinned. Sin already existed in the world before there was any law, even though sin is not reckoned when there is no law. Nonetheless death reigned over all from Adam to Moses, even over those whose sin was not the breaking of a commandment, as Adam's was. He prefigured the One who was to come…

There is no comparison between the free gift and the offence. If death came to many through the offence of one man, how much greater an effect the grace of God has had, coming to so many and so plentifully as a free gift through the one man Jesus Christ! Again, there is no comparison between the gift and the offence of one man. One single offence brought condemnation, but now, after many offences, have come the free gift and so acquittal! It was by one man's offence that death came to reign over all, but how much greater the reign in life of those who receive the fullness of grace and the gift of saving justice, through the one man, Jesus Christ. One man's offence brought condemnation on all humanity; and one man's good act has brought justification and life to all humanity. Just as by one man's disobedience many were made sinners, so by one man's obedience are many to be made upright. When law came on the scene, it was to multiply the offences. But however much sin increased, grace was always greater; so that as sin's reign brought death, so grace was to rule through saving justice that leads to eternal life through Jesus Christ our Lord.

❦

In a second explanation of Christ's saving work, Paul lays it out not in the cultic terms of the old Law, but in terms of Christ's obedience. The obedience of Christ, the second Adam, undoes the disobedience of the first Adam.

The first Adam is the image or icon of humanity. The story of the fall of Adam and Eve is not a story of what happened long ago so much as the analysis of what happens every day when we are tempted and fall. It is the analysis of our self-will, our disobedience, then our naked shame when we realize how inexcusable that was and how defenceless we are, and finally of God's continued love despite everything that we can do. We are subject to death not because of the sin of someone else long ago, but because of our own sin, 'because everyone has sinned'. Adam's sin is seen as the beginning of sin, which spread to all people, since all people are born into the sinful and distorted world, and we react to the sin of others with our own sin.

This can be overcome only by an obedience which is

ours—that is, human—but is greater than ours, namely that of Christ, the second Adam. It was not Christ's blood in itself that redeemed us, but Christ's obedience to the point of blood. Christ's obedience on the cross was the apex of the loving union of Jesus with his Father, the moment at which he was most perfectly at one with the will with his Father. It had seemed that his attempt to spread the sovereignty of God had failed. His band of disciples, forming the new Israel, had deserted, betrayed or denied him, and nothing was left. Yet he still carried on in obedience to his Father's will. The centurion's words acknowledge this when he says, 'In truth this man was son of God' (Matthew 27:54). As a devoted and loving son behaves to his devoted and loving father, so Jesus is united to the Father. This was the high point of all human existence, which the Father recognized by vindicating Christ in the resurrection.

*Lord Jesus, help me to learn obedience to you, even as you learnt obedience to your Father.*

# 20

# Saturated With Christ

ROMANS 6:3–11

You cannot have forgotten that all of us, when we were baptised into Christ Jesus, were baptised into his death. So by our baptism into his death we were buried with him, so that as Christ was raised from the dead by the Father's glorious power, we too should begin living a new life. If we have been joined to him by dying a death like his, so we shall be by a resurrection like his; realizing that our former self was crucified with him, so that the self which belonged to sin should be destroyed and we should be freed from the slavery of sin. Someone who has died, of course, no longer has to answer for sin.

But we believe that, if we died with Christ, then we shall live with him too. We know that Christ has been raised from the dead and will never die again. Death has no power over him any more. For by dying, he is dead to sin once and for all, and now the life that he lives is life with God. In the same way, you must see yourselves as being dead to sin but alive for God in Christ in Jesus.

❖ ❖

What has Christ's great act of obedience to do with me? How can it benefit me? Paul's answer is that by baptism I have been dipped into Christ's death. The Greek *baptizo* means to 'dip'. Baptism is the expression of faith, the expression of where I put my trust. By baptism in faith into Christ's death, I express my total trust in Christ's death and resurrection. So I have been dipped into his death and come up saturated, soaked through with Christ, into his resurrection. Paul now uses a string of images to show how this 'saturation' works, and how I have been clothed with Christ and his power, indeed with his very life. I now live with Christ's life.

There is, however, still a difference: Paul is hesitant about speaking of our resurrection in the same breath as Christ's resurrection. Although we *have died* with Christ, we *shall be* raised with Christ. Paul is happy to say that we have begun living a life with Christ, we have been freed from slavery to sin, we have been reconciled to God, but he will not say that we have been saved. Only once (8:24) does he say that, and then it is qualified by 'in hope', which again turns it into a future tense. This coincides with the expression here translated 'joined to', that Christians are *symfytoi* with Christ, growing into Christ as the two parts of a broken bone grow back into each other again. For, as he says in 2 Corinthians, we *are being* transformed in Christ; the process is not yet complete. Only in the later post-Pauline letters does it say that we have been raised with Christ, qualified by the statement that this is still to be made manifest in our bodies.

The consequence of dying with Christ's death is that I am freed from slavery to sin, and am the slave only of obedience, which is a very different matter. For Paul, the great evil pair is sin and death, and, for him, sin plus law equals death. In being freed from one, I am freed from the whole trio.

*Lord, enable me to live with your life ever more fully and so be wholly transformed into your image.*

# 21

# The Inner Struggle

ROMANS 7:15–25

I do not understand my own behaviour; I do not act as I mean to, but I do things that I hate. While I am acting as I do not want to, I still acknowledge the Law as good, so it is not myself acting, but the sin which lives in me. And really, I know of nothing good living in me—in my natural self, that is—for though the will to do what is good is in me, the power to do it is not: the good thing I want to do, I never do; the evil thing which I do not want—that is what I do. But every time I do what I do not want to, then it is not myself acting, but the sin that lives in me.

So I find this rule: that for me, where I want to do nothing but good, evil is close at my side. In my inmost self I dearly love God's law, but I see that acting on my body there is a different law which battles against the law in my mind. So I am brought to be a prisoner of that law of sin which lives inside my body.

What a wretched man I am! Who will rescue me from this body doomed to death? God—thanks be to him—through Jesus Christ our Lord.

So it is that I myself with my mind obey the law of God, but in my disordered nature I obey the law of sin.

Not so fast! Not so fast! Here Paul pulls back. It is all very well to talk about being freed from sin, but is that the reality that I feel? Paul reflects sadly and bitterly on the experience that is all too familiar to us: 'the good thing I want to do, I never do'. Theoretically, I have been freed from sin to live with Christ's life, but, despite this, I know only too well that I continue in sin. I may have been freed from the Law, in the sense of the Jewish Law, but I am still subject to the law of sin. To paraphrase a little, in my rational mind or my intentions I obey the law of God, I intend to do God's will; but in my human nature, the 'flesh', my natural inclinations, I obey the law of sin.

Paul is speaking not only of temptations that we would call 'fleshly'—lust, drunkenness, greed—though everyone knows that the mind is involved in these too (the mind has been described as the chief sexual organ). Paul is speaking also of the 'higher' natural tendencies, such as jealousy, malice, bad temper. Remember the list in Galatians 5! What, then, does it mean to be living with Christ's life, inspired by his Spirit, if the Spirit is ineffective? Perhaps it means only that the transformation is a long process and that human nature does not suddenly go away.

Paul is an orator who has enjoyed a rhetorical training. This is often apparent in the letters. He loves playing with words. Frequently in the letters he uses the technique called 'diatribe', which consists in a volley of questions to which he supplies imaginary answers: 'Should we say…? Out of the question! Or…? No, indeed!' Here he is playing with the word 'law', sometimes meaning the Jewish Law or Torah, sometimes God's law in the wider sense of the will of God, and sometimes the law of the flesh, in the sense of natural inclinations. Sometimes he means the law of the Spirit, and by this he means the inspiration of Christ's Spirit living within us and guiding our actions.

*Lord, save me from myself and strengthen your life within me.*

# 22

# The Glory to Come

ROMANS 8:18–27

In my estimation, all that we suffer in the present time is nothing in comparison with the glory which is destined to be disclosed for us, for the whole creation is waiting with eagerness for the children of God to be revealed. It was not for its own purposes that creation had frustration imposed on it, but for the purposes of him who imposed it—with the intention that the whole creation itself might be freed from its slavery to corruption and brought into the same glorious freedom as the children of God. We are well aware that the whole creation, until this time, has been groaning in labour pains. And not only that: we too, who have the first-fruits of the Spirit, even we are groaning inside ourselves, waiting with eagerness for our bodies to be set free. In hope, we already have salvation; in hope, not visibly present, or we should not be hoping—nobody goes on hoping for something which is already visible. But having this hope for what we cannot yet see, we are able to wait for it with persevering confidence.

And as well as this, the Spirit too comes to help us in our weakness, for, when we do not know how to pray properly, then the Spirit personally makes our petitions for us in groans that cannot be put into words; and he who can see into all hearts knows what the Spirit means because the prayers that the Spirit makes for God's holy people are always in accordance with the mind of God.

❧ ☙

At the beginning of his letter Paul had said that, by the fall, human beings exchanged the glory of the immortal God for an imitation (1:23). This involved not only human beings but the whole of creation, which had 'frustration imposed on it' (8:20). The loss of God's glory by human beings disrupted the whole harmony of creation with God: the divine glory could no longer continue to bathe creation in its light. Now the reversal in Christ also implicates the whole of creation, so that the whole of creation is to be freed from corruption and brought into glorious freedom. As the sin of Adam destroyed or destroys the whole harmony of creation, making childbirth painful and work toilsome, so life in Christ restores it. We are only the firstfruits, the presage of full restoration. The transformation being worked by the Spirit of Christ affects all creation.

One effect of this partial transformation is that we cannot fully articulate our prayers or properly express our desires to God. We cannot yet see the fullness of the objective we desire, and the Spirit groans within us for what we cannot yet put into words. This is a great comfort in prayer: even though we cannot yet pray properly, with full devotion and concentration, the Spirit makes up for our faulty efforts.

Paul concludes this account of the process of salvation with an inspiring hymn to the love of God: 'If God is for us, who can be against us? ... Neither... the heights nor the depths, nor any created thing whatever, will be able to come between us and the love of God' (see 8:31–39). What an unforgettable climax! It prepares and leads into Paul's agonized reflections on the situation of his beloved brothers, the Jews who have not accepted Christ (Romans 9—11). How is it that they too will eventually be saved? The unshakeable love of God applies to the Jews also. How it will happen he cannot explain, but that it will happen he is certain. This will be confirmed by yet another wonderful Pauline hymn: 'How rich and deep are the wisdom and the knowledge of God!' (see 11:33–36).

*Lord, bring your glory into being among us, that we may recognize and once again acknowledge your full sovereignty.*

# 23

# Christ is not Divided

## 1 CORINTHIANS 1:10–18

Brothers, I urge you, in the name of our Lord Jesus Christ, not to have factions among yourselves but all to be in agreement in what you profess; so that you are perfectly united in your beliefs and judgments. From what Chloe's people have been telling me about you, brothers, it is clear that there are serious differences among you. What I mean is this: every one of you is declaring, 'I belong to Paul,' or 'I belong to Apollos,' or 'I belong to Cephas,' or 'I belong to Christ.' Has Christ been split up? Was it Paul that was crucified for you, or was it in Paul's name that you were baptized? I am thankful I did not baptize any of you, except Crispus and Gaius, so that no one can say that you were baptized in my name. Yes, I did baptize the family of Stephanas, too; but besides these I do not think I baptized anyone.

After all, Christ sent me not to baptize, but to preach the gospel; and not by means of wisdom of language, wise words which would make the cross of Christ pointless. The message of the cross is folly for those who are on the way to ruin, but for those of us who are on the road to salvation it is the power of God.

In Paul's day Corinth was a boom city. It had been sacked and destroyed in 146BC by the Romans, but its geographical position was such that it proved indispensible and it was refounded a century later by Julius Caesar. By Paul's time it was again at the height of its powers. It sat astride a narrow neck of land, where the Corinthian canal now runs, with a harbour each side, between which goods were transported by land. It was a flourishing port, bursting with labourers and tycoons. It was also host to the popular biennial Isthmian Games, which attracted competitors and spectators from all over Greece and beyond, and which were more celebrated than the nearby Olympic Games. When Paul founded the Christian community there, he set up no human authority structure, for the Spirit was vigorously at work. This would be the cause of some trouble later!

A woman called Chloe sent messengers to Paul at Ephesus with a letter asking various questions, and in his answering letter Paul deals first with these matters. They also brought news about the community. The Christian community had split into factions. Some retained their loyalty to Paul, their father in Christ. Others claimed to follow Apollos, a Jewish Christian preacher from Alexandria, probably rather intellectual. Others preferred Cephas. As we have already seen, this is the Aramaic name for Peter, and we may guess that this was the group that followed the Judaizing party with which Paul had had such trouble at Antioch and in Galatia.

Paul responds by expressing his horror at the divisiveness of it all. Christ cannot be split up. All were baptized into the name of Jesus—that is, into the company or body of Jesus. The early Christians were known as those over whom the name, the power, of Jesus had been pronounced. They were not followers of Paul, Apollos or Peter. Despite the prayer of Jesus that all might be one, there were from the very beginning strong convictions in the Christian Church, which led to divisions. Paul's response should be a model for ours.

*Lord, grant your Church the tolerance and understanding that will bring together all your disciples in peace and harmony.*

# 24

# True Wisdom

## 1 CORINTHIANS 1:21–27

Since in the wisdom of God the world was unable to recognize God through wisdom, it was God's own pleasure to save believers through the folly of the gospel. While the Jews demand miracles and the Greeks look for wisdom, we are preaching a crucified Christ: to the Jews an obstacle they cannot get over, to the gentiles foolishness, but to those who have been called, whether they are Jews or Greeks, a Christ who is both the power of God and the wisdom of God. God's folly is wiser than human wisdom, and God's weakness is stronger than human strength. Consider, brothers, how you were called; not many of you are wise by human standards, not many influential, not many from noble families. No, God chose those who by human standards are fools to shame the wise; he chose those who by human standards are weak to shame the strong.

❧ ❧

Why does Paul drop suddenly into an attack on human wisdom? There are suggestions throughout the letter that there was a degree of arrogance among the Corinthians. Paul is quite uncharacteristically sarcastic about the Corinthians, saying again and again that there are not many among them who are wise or well-born, that they are like children who still have to be fed on milk rather than normal food. There is also the matter of the slogans: Paul seems to quote self-confident slogans, like 'For me everything is permissible' (6:12), which the Corinthians must have produced and which he moderates or contradicts. All this must have been galling to the proud among them as it was read out publicly in their assembly! The second letter to the Corinthians shows that this first letter caused considerable upset and revulsion against Paul in the community. There were some who needed a good deal of persuading and cajoling before they learnt the lesson. And we are not bound to believe that, in his attempts to drive home the lesson, Paul was always the most tactful of men!

Positively, however, this attack on human wisdom provides us with two invaluable lessons. Firstly, there is the lesson that God's system of values does not necessarily coincide with ours. Human values, human distinction and success are not the chief values in God's eyes. Rather, throughout the scriptures we find that God favours and protects the poor, the weak, the sick and the underprivileged, and that God's friends must do the same.

Secondly, Paul introduces the invaluable contrast that, whereas the Greeks may value wisdom, no doubt in the form of their own well-developed philosophical systems, the true wisdom of God can only be found in Christ. This looks back to the Wisdom literature of the Old Testament, where God's wisdom is praised as the reflection and outworking of God in the world. Wisdom is the mediator between God and creation, the agent of God in the world. It is by his wisdom that God creates. Divine Wisdom offers a banquet of God's good things and insistently invites all to join in the feast. Now we see that Christ is this Wisdom of God, by whom God creates and who calls all people to a share in God's banquet.

*You who are Wisdom, Lord, grant me your true wisdom, that I may see the world as you see it and appreciate the values that are yours.*

# 25

# The Temple of the Spirit

## 1 CORINTHIANS 6:12–19

'For me everything is permissible'; maybe, but not everything does good. True, for me everything is permissible, but I am determined not to be dominated by anything. Foods are for the stomach, and the stomach is for foods; and God will destroy them both. But the body is not for sexual immorality; it is for the Lord, and the Lord is for the body. God raised up the Lord and he will raise us up too by his power. Do you not realize that your bodies are members of Christ's body; do you think one can take parts of Christ's body and join them to the body of a prostitute? Out of the question! Or do you not realize that anyone who attaches himself to a prostitute is one body with her, since the two, as it is said, become one flesh. But anyone who attaches himself to the Lord is one spirit with him.

Keep away from sexual immorality. All other sins that people may commit are done outside the body; but the sexually immoral person sins against his own body. Do you not realize that your body is the temple of the Holy Spirit, who is in you and whom you received from God?

This passage starts with one of the slogans that the Corinthian 'know-alls' seem to have flung at Paul—or at any rate at those who tried to restrain them: 'For me everything is permissible'. Paul had taught that the Jewish Law need not be observed. Had they concluded from his necessarily short and incomplete teaching that there are no laws, no limits and no restrictions of behaviour? Another slogan may be the catchy phrase, 'Foods are for the stomach and the stomach is for foods', with the implication that it does not matter what you eat, brushing aside the scruples of some who were hesitant about eating food sacrificed to idols (chs. 8—10). Paul does not, on the whole, lay down rules for Christian behaviour, since he is convinced that the Spirit of Christ will guide those who commit themselves to him. There is, however, room for some moral teaching to bring out the applications of Christianity.

As always, it is not merely Paul's conclusions that are valuable but also his principles. In this case, the presence of Christ in the Christian is so real to him that he sees the Christian's body as Christ's own. If I defile my body, I defile Christ's body, for my body is Christ's, right to the fingertips. It is not just a vague or 'spiritual' presence but a total and physical presence, including my sexuality. Everything I do involves Christ: for good or for bad, Christ is always there with me.

This is what Paul means when he says that our bodies are the temple of the Holy Spirit. For faithful Jews, the temple was the dwelling place of God. In John's Gospel Jesus had said of himself, 'Destroy this Temple, and in three days I will raise it up' (2:19). Now Paul applies it to all Christians, for all live in the Spirit and life of Christ. As Jesus had said at the last supper, 'Remain in me, as I in you' (John 15:4). The honour of this presence and the responsibility it confers on all Christians are daunting: we carry Christ with us.

*Lord, remain in me and guide me to revere your presence in my body and all its actions.*

# 26

# The Time is Short

1 CORINTHIANS 7:29–35

What I mean, brothers, is that the time has become limited, and from now on, those who have spouses should live as though they had none; and those who mourn as though they were not mourning; those who enjoy life as though they did not enjoy it; those who have been buying property as though they had no possessions; and those who are involved with the world as though they were people not engrossed in it. Because this world as we know it is passing away.

I should like you to have your minds free from all worry. The unmarried man gives his mind to the Lord's affairs and to how he can please the Lord; but the man who is married gives his mind to the affairs of this world and to how he can please his wife, and he is divided in mind. So, too, the unmarried woman, and the virgin, gives her mind to the Lord's affairs and to being holy in body and spirit; but the married woman gives her mind to the affairs of this world and to how she can please her husband. I am saying this only to help you, not to put a bridle on you, but so that everything is as it should be, and you are able to give your undivided attention to the Lord.

❧ ❧

As we saw in the letters to the Thessalonians, the final coming of Christ in glory was a very real hope for Paul and the early Christians. 'The Kingdom of God has drawn near' was the cry from John the Baptist onwards. Jesus taught that there was a pressing need to make a decision. It could not be put off; it was urgent! This attitude cooled only gradually among Christians. Matthew, the second Gospel to be written, presupposes that the last judgment is a pressing but comparatively distant reality, whereas in Mark (the first to be written) this is less clear. Paul is, of course, writing his letters some decades before any of the Gospels. He sees the death throes of the world as an occasion of agony, turmoil and cosmic disturbance, and probably moral chaos as well. If children are born only to be engulfed in this horrific turmoil, it may be better not to bring them into the world at all and to remain unmarried. Would it be fair to bring children into the world in the knowledge that they were to be engulfed in the horrors of an atom bomb or a tsunami?

The fact that this turmoil did not happen, or at least has not yet happened, could be considered disturbing. Did Paul get it wrong? Was he, then, not inspired? The answer to this teaches an important truth: we must look at the whole course of revelation in the Bible, not merely a part, for individual truths become clearer in the course of revelation. Take, for example, the teaching on revenge. The Old Testament limited revenge to '[Only] eye for eye' (Leviticus 24:20), but Jesus went further and forbade his followers to take any revenge at all (Matthew 5:38–39).

So Paul's teaching on virginity needs adjustment. We do not see the end of the world as an imminent threat but the Christian must see the values of the world as limited and at best provisional. The happiness of married life is not definitive; joy in possessions is not permanent. Our life is centred on a deeper joy.

*Lord, help me to value the joys of this world as provisional and concentrate on the one thing necessary.*

# 27

# Respect!

## 1 CORINTHIANS 8:5–13

Though there are so-called gods, in the heavens or on earth—and there are plenty of gods and plenty of lords—yet for us there is only one God, the Father from whom all things come and for whom we exist, and one Lord, Jesus Christ, through whom all things come and through whom we exist.

However, not everybody has this knowledge. There are some in whose consciences false gods still play such a part that they take the food as though it had been dedicated to a god; then their conscience, being vulnerable, is defiled. But of course food cannot make us acceptable to God; we lose nothing by not eating it, we gain nothing by eating it. Only be careful that this freedom of yours does not in any way turn into an obstacle to trip those who are vulnerable. Suppose someone sees you, who have the knowledge, sitting eating in the temple of some false god, do you not think that his conscience, vulnerable as it is, may be encouraged to eat foods dedicated to false gods? And then it would be through your knowledge that this brother for whom Christ died, vulnerable as he is, has been lost. So, sinning against your brothers and wounding their vulnerable consciences, you would be sinning against Christ. That is why, if food can be the cause of a brother's downfall, I will never eat meat any more, rather than cause my brother's downfall.

❦ ❧

We begin with a wonderful statement of the position of Christ. Paul is commenting on the basic confession of faith, recited twice daily by every faithful Jew, 'The Lord our God is one God' (Deuteronomy 6:4, author's translation). No, says Paul. For us there is one God, the Father, and one Lord, Jesus Christ—the Father from whom everything exists and the Lord through whom everything exists. So he explains what it means to call Jesus 'Lord'.

In this second half of the letter, Paul is replying to questions put to him. The replies all begin 'Now about...' (7:1; 8:1; 12:1). One of the questions concerned a social and financial difficulty at Corinth. Since the priests of the Roman temples could not eat all the meat that they sacrificed, the spare meat was sold off cheap in the market. Could Christians eat it, either buying it themselves or sharing it at someone else's table? Some thought the meat was defiled because it had been offered to idols. Paul's reply is that idols are nothing, since the gods they represent do not exist. Therefore, meat that has been offered to them is unchanged and not defiled.

This neat and succinct answer is not the most important part of the argument. A more important factor is Paul's consideration for the conscience of others. He expects that some will not see the force of the argument, and lays down the cardinal principle that every person has a right to their own conscientious opinion: no one is to be forced, or even influenced by example, to act against their conscience. How far can this go? The fundamental principle is that the rights and conscience of others must be respected.

The principle of conscience has not always been observed in the Church: there have been forcible 'conversions' on the principle that 'error has no rights'. Here too the teaching of the Church has developed and become more respectful of individuals. But it is all there in Paul.

*May I learn to respect the conscience of others, and uphold their right to think differently from me.*

# 28

# Advice to Christian Women

### 1 CORINTHIANS 11:3–11

But I should like you to understand that the head of every man is Christ, the head of woman is man, and the head of Christ is God. For any man to pray or to prophesy with his head covered shows disrespect for his head. And for a woman to pray or prophesy with her head uncovered shows disrespect for her head; it is exactly the same as if she had her hair shaved off. Indeed, if a woman does go without a veil, she should have her hair cut off too; but if it is a shameful thing for a woman to have her hair cut off or shaved off, then she should wear a veil.

But for a man it is not right to have his head covered, since he is the image of God and reflects God's glory; but woman is the reflection of man's glory. For man did not come from woman; no, woman came from man; nor was man created for the sake of woman, but woman for the sake of man: and this is why it is right for a woman to wear on her head a sign of the authority over her, because of the angels. However, in the Lord, though woman is nothing without man, man is nothing without woman.

Paul is often condemned as a male chauvinist for this passage, in which he considers that woman was created for the sake of man and quite definitely not the opposite. Such condemnation is unjustified. In this passage he insists that, if women are to speak in the public assembly, they must have the proper headdress, a very sensitive point in the ancient world. Later in the letter comes a passage which seems to say that women may not speak at all in the assembly of the church (14:34–35). That contradicts the present passage, and various explanations have been given: perhaps it was added later by another author, or perhaps Paul is quoting a Corinthian objection to his ruling. Certainly it is followed by the rather sarcastic, 'Do you really think that you are the source of the word of God?' (v. 36), which seems to negate the preceding comments.

In any case, it is quite clear that Paul had a due regard for women and their place in the Christian community, though he was also, of course, a man of his times. Women could not take part in politics or many other public functions, but in the Jewish communities scattered round the Roman world there are many inscriptions which show that women could be elected president over the local assembly and its board of elders. According to Acts (16:15), the first person Paul baptized in Europe was a woman, Lydia. Then he worked closely with a married couple, Priscilla and Aquila, and often mentions the wife before the husband. It was a woman, Chloe, who sent her messengers to him at Ephesus and occasioned this letter. It was a woman, Phoebe, who carried the letter to the Romans. In Romans 16 Paul is unstinting in his greetings and praise to various women of the Roman community, calling Junia 'distinguished among the apostles' (v. 7).

So women had an important part in the first Christian assemblies. Admittedly, there were no women among the Twelve, the foundation stones of Jesus' new Israel, but at least one of the evangelists, Luke, is careful to put women on a par with men and gives special honour to Mary, the mother of Jesus.

*Lord, save us from narrow-mindedness, keep us from being judgmental and make us appreciative of the talents and goodness of others.*

# 29

# The Body of Christ

## 1 CORINTHIANS 12:4–15

There are many different gifts, but it is always the same Spirit; there are many different ways of serving, but it is always the same Lord. There are many different forms of activity, but in everybody it is the same God who is at work in them all. The particular manifestation of the Spirit granted to each one is to be used for the general good. To one is given from the Spirit the gift of utterance expressing wisdom; to another the gift of utterance expressing knowledge, in accordance with the same Spirit; to another, faith, from the same Spirit; and to another, the gifts of healing, through this one Spirit; to another, the working of miracles; to another, prophecy; to another, the power of distinguishing spirits; to one, the gift of different tongues and to another, the interpretation of tongues. But at work in all these is one and the same Spirit, distributing them at will to each individual.

For as with the human body which is a unity although it has many parts—all the parts of the body, though many, still making up one single body—so it is with Christ. We were baptized into one body in a single Spirit, Jews as well as Greeks, slaves as well as free men, and we were all given the same Spirit to drink. And indeed the body consists not of one member but of many. If the foot were to say, 'I am not a hand and so I do not belong to the body,' it does not belong to the body any the less for that.

❮ ❯

We now come to the most remarkable feature of the Christian community at Corinth, the gifts of the Spirit. The Spirit of the Lord was at work in them in all kinds of ways. We need not regard all these ways as strictly miraculous in the sense of 'against nature', though they must have been manifestations of the power of the Lord in the sense of 'beyond nature'. They had powers of healing at least in the sense of the healing touch, the healing word that the Christian can give to those who are wounded and need comfort. They had powers of prophecy, not necessarily in the sense of foreseeing the future, but of seeing a situation with real clarity as God sees it and being able to interpret it with penetrating truth, giving people encouragement and reassurance (14:3). Among these gifts was 'speaking in tongues', perhaps a bubbling over of prayer into language that needed interpretation. Paul is cool about this. He mentions it last of all and is wary of the disorder it can bring and the bad impression to outsiders who think it mere gibberish (vv. 4–19). Besides these, there are the more functional gifts of the apostolate and of teaching (12:28).

The trouble was that, in this divided community, people were fixated on the phenomena of the gifts themselves rather than on the function of those gifts. Paul insists that each of the gifts has its part to play in building up the community, and it is this function rather than the gift itself that is important. Here he introduces the image of the body: each member of the body has its own unique part to play, a role of special value but directed to the harmony of the body as a whole. They should value each member as making a unique contribution to the whole.

Paul uses a figure here that was already a familiar image in politics and in popular philosophy. What is unique about Paul's usage is that, for him, the Christian body is Christ. Nowhere else in this popular usage is the body described as being the body of a person.

*Lord, let me value my abilities and those of others as your gifts, given for building up your body, which is the community.*

# 30

# The Meaning of Love

## 1 CORINTHIANS 13:1–9

Though I command languages both human and angelic—if I speak without love, I am no more than a gong booming or a cymbal clashing. And though I have the power of prophecy, to penetrate all mysteries and knowledge, and though I have all the faith necessary to move mountains—if I am without love, I am nothing. Though I should give away to the poor all that I possess, and even give up my body to be burned—if I am without love, it will do me no good whatever.

Love is always patient and kind; love is never jealous; love is not boastful or conceited, it is never rude and never seeks its own advantage, it does not take offence or store up grievances. Love does not rejoice at wrongdoing, but finds its joy in the truth. It is always ready to make allowances, to trust, to hope and to endure whatever comes.

Love never comes to an end. But if there are prophecies, they will be done away with; if tongues, they will fall silent; and if knowledge, it will be done away with. For we know only imperfectly, and we prophesy imperfectly.

Possibly better known and more frequently read in public than any other passage in scripture, this analysis of the true meaning of love never loses its freshness and value. It is, of course, not Paul's invention, for this Christian concept of love builds on the Jewish concept of family love—not a self-seeking search for satisfaction but a love turned toward the advantage and interests of others. It is a profound and generous love, relying not on superficial harmony or mere personal liking of one individual for another, but on responsiveness to needs—whatever my feelings are for that person. In Judaism, members of the family were positively obliged to help out other family members in difficulties, an obligation that forged the family unity and bound the family together. Paul sees the generous and unitive power of love in building up the community to be the real purpose of the gifts that the Corinthians seem to have regarded as personal gifts to themselves and a matter for self-congratulation and pride.

The earlier part of the passage suggests a challenging series of tests, which we may apply to see whether or not our love is real. Am I really patient or is my generosity short-lived? Do I boast of my acts of 'kindness' to boost my own reputation? Three very testing questions: do I store up grievances for a day when I can repay them? Am I delighted when someone else is caught out in wrongdoing? Do I take quick offence or do I look for reasons why another person may have been hurtful, expressing the sort of discerning understanding that I would expect from others?

The later part celebrates the permanence of love. It is

a long-term quality in individuals and is also the quality that gives permanence to a society. Civilizations have failed when service has given way to self-interest and self-aggrandisement. Paul, however, is thinking especially of the final company in happiness with God, where love alone remains: 'As it is, these remain: faith, hope and love, the three of them; and the greatest of them is love' (13:13).

*Lord God, you are generous love itself, seeking no recompense. Grant me a share in that supreme quality of love.*

# 31

# The Risen Life

## 1 CORINTHIANS 15:35–44

Someone may ask: How are dead people raised, and what sort of body do they have when they come? How foolish! What you sow must die before it is given new life; and what you sow is not the body that is to be, but only a bare grain, of wheat I dare say, or some other kind; it is God who gives it the sort of body that he has chosen for it, and for each kind of seed its own kind of body. Not all flesh is the same flesh: there is human flesh; animals have another kind of flesh, birds another and fish yet another. Then there are heavenly bodies and earthly bodies; the heavenly have a splendour of their own, and the earthly a different splendour. The sun has its own splendour, the moon another splendour, and the stars yet another splendour; and the stars differ among themselves in splendour. It is the same too with the resurrection of the dead: what is sown is perishable, but what is raised is imperishable; what is sown is contemptible but what is raised is glorious; what is sown is weak, but what is raised is powerful; what is sown is a natural body, and what is raised is a spiritual body. If there is a natural body, there is a spiritual body too.

This passage is of central importance for the Christian teaching on life after death and on the resurrection. After Paul has rebuked various excesses among the Corinthians and has answered their questions, he goes on to show that the manifestations of the Spirit among them are only the beginning. They still have to await the final transformation in the Spirit, when Christians will follow Christ, the second Adam and the 'first-fruits' of the resurrection (15:20–23), into risen life. What form will this life take?

Firstly, he counsels, there is no point in trying to imagine what sort of body we will have (v. 35–36). There is no answer to this question. It will be a real body but not with the same qualities as the bodies we now have. In the Jewish concept of a human being, there is no room for the Greek distinction of body and soul: there is no separable soul, for the living person is an animated body. The life force, that is, the soul, is what makes the difference between a living person and a hunk of meat.

Secondly, there will be continuity between me now and me as I shall be in the transformation (v. 37–38). The wheat grain that dies produces wheat, not brambles. Indeed, if there were no continuity, the resurrection to life would be of no interest to me. I would not be there to appreciate it! Thirdly, there is an analogy (v. 39–41). Not all bodies are the same 'body'. Not all splendours are the same splendour. So the body as it will be is not exactly the same as the body which I have (or which I am) now. It will be a body but in a different way.

What will the difference be (v. 42–44)? There will be no corruption, only the incorruptibility of God. There will be nothing contemptible or shameful, only the glory of God. There will be no weakness, only the strength of God. The life principle will be not the human soul but the Spirit of God. We will be transferred into the sphere of God and in these ways transformed by the divine life.

*We cannot fully understand, Lord, what this risen life will be. Enough that it will be life with you and in your glory.*

# 32

# Saying Yes to God

## 2 CORINTHIANS 1:15–20

It was with this assurance that I had been meaning to come to you first, so that you would benefit doubly; both to visit you on my way to Macedonia, and then to return to you again from Macedonia, so that you could set me on my way to Judaea. Since that was my purpose, do you think I lightly changed my mind? Or that my plans are based on ordinary human promptings and I have in my mind Yes, yes at the same time as No, no? As surely as God is trustworthy, what we say to you is not both Yes and No. The Son of God, Jesus Christ, who was proclaimed to you by us, that is, by me and by Silvanus and Timothy, was never Yes-and-No; his nature is all Yes. For in him is found the Yes to all God's promises and therefore it is 'through him' that we answer 'Amen' to give praise to God.

After the first letter to the Corinthians, relations between Paul and the community were stormy. Not surprising, in view of his firm criticisms and his often sarcastic tone! They cannot have enjoyed listening to the first part of the letter. However, Paul promised to visit them again on his way to and from Macedonia, in the north of Greece—or so they thought. In the end, Paul did not visit them and now has to explain that he intended to visit them but never promised to do so. He does not renege on his promises!

This was all a bit unfortunate but it provides the occasion for this valuable outline of Christ as the 'Amen' of the Father. 'Amen' comes from the Hebrew word meaning 'firmness', 'truth', 'stability'. Its basic sense is to confirm, 'That goes for me too'—for example, at the end of a prayer. You say the prayer and, if I agree, I say 'Amen!' Or at the end of an oath, when you make the oath and I accept the oath for myself too, I cry out 'Amen!' Hence the Jewish saying, 'Only a fool says "Amen" to his own prayer.' One valuable sideproduct is that it shows that Paul thought in Hebrew—as one would expect from someone who was trained in Jerusalem under Rabbi Gamaliel II, one of the greatest teachers of his time.

The basis of all Paul's thinking and expectation was the promises that God made to Abraham in Genesis 12. Jesus is the 'Amen' to these promises because he is their fulfilment. He is no half-hearted or wavering fulfilment, no 'Yes-and-No', but a whole-hearted 'Yes', the fulfilment to which all the promises looked forward. Paul attests that he, too, is just as firm and does not back out of his promises. In fact, it appears from the letter that Paul was quite right not to risk a confrontation. Instead, he sent Timothy, whom they insulted. After that, he sent them a biting reproof, which he says it pained him to write (2:4), and after that sent this more peaceful letter to smooth things down.

*You are the 'Amen' of the Father's promises, Lord Jesus. Grant that I may take these promises to myself, and so join in your 'Amen'.*

# 33

# Undaunted Suffering

## 2 CORINTHIANS 6:4–18

In everything we prove ourselves authentic servants of God; by resolute perseverance in times of hardships, difficulties and distress; when we are flogged or sent to prison or mobbed; labouring, sleepless, starving; in purity, in knowledge, in patience, in kindness; in the Holy Spirit, in a love free of affectation; in the word of truth and in the power of God; by using the weapons of uprightness for attack and for defence: in times of honour or disgrace, blame or praise; taken for impostors and yet we are genuine; unknown and yet we are acknowledged; dying, and yet here we are, alive; scourged but not executed; in pain yet always full of joy; poor and yet making many people rich; having nothing, and yet owning everything.

People of Corinth, we have spoken frankly and opened our heart to you. Any distress you feel is not on our side; the distress is in your own selves. In fair exchange— I speak as though to children of mine—you must open your hearts too.

Do not harness yourselves in an uneven team with unbelievers; how can uprightness and law-breaking be partners, or what can light and darkness have in common? How can Christ come to an agreement with Beliar and what sharing can there be between a believer and an unbeliever? The temple of God cannot compromise with false gods, and that is what we are—the temple of the living God. We have God's word for it: I shall fix my home among them and live among them; I will be their God and they will be my people. Get away from them, purify yourselves, says the Lord. Do not touch anything unclean, and then I shall welcome you. I shall be father to you, and you will be sons and daughters to me, says the almighty Lord.

❦

Our passage begins with one of Paul's most noble announcements of his courageous undaunted sufferings for Christ. It is because of these sufferings that he regards himself as the Servant of Christ, as Christ is the Servant of God. It is his perseverance in suffering that gives him an authority greater than the authority of the rival 'super-apostles' who seek to undermine him at Corinth.

Then comes an unexpected little piece (6:14—7:1), which seems alien to its context. It is a warning against any compromise with evil, but occurs between two very intimate and affectionate passages from Paul to his 'dear children' at Corinth. Various touches seem uncharacteristic of the Paul we know: he never calls the tempter 'Beliar' (v. 15) but normally uses such expressions as 'the Evil One'; neither is he normally concerned about ritual purity, as he appears to be here (v. 17; 7:1). Another striking factor is that these verses have a definite similarity to the writings of the Dead Sea Scrolls found at Qumran. There we find the same concern to separate from evildoers, which was why the Qumran community settled out in the desert by the Dead Sea. In contrast, Paul is normally more concerned with the conquest of evil by the power and Spirit of Christ. The same opposition between light and darkness is also prominent (v. 14).

So, one suggestion is that Paul did not write these words at all. Another suggestion is that this passage is Paul's first letter of all to the Corinthians, the letter he mentions in 1 Corinthians 5:9, warning 'that you should have nothing to do with people living immoral lives'. It seems odd that this letter should have been stuffed into the middle of the larger letter, but we do not know how Paul's letters came to be collected. Perhaps 2 Corinthians is in fact a collection of several shorter letters to the Corinthians.

*Lord, give me the same perseverance and cheerfulness as Paul when I have to suffer for your name.*

# 34

# Remember the Poor

## 2 CORINTHIANS 8:1–9

Next, brothers, we will tell you of the grace of God which has been granted to the churches of Macedonia, and how, throughout continual ordeals of hardship, their unfailing joy and their intense poverty have overflowed in a wealth of generosity on their part. I can testify that it was of their own accord that they made their gift, which was not merely as far as their resources would allow, but well beyond their resources; and they had kept imploring us most insistently for the privilege of a share in the fellowship of service to God's holy people— it was not something that we expected of them, but it began by their offering themselves to the Lord and to us at the prompting of the will of God. In the end we urged Titus, since he had already made a beginning, also to bring this work of generosity to completion among you. More, as you are rich in everything—faith, eloquence, understanding, concern for everything, and love for us too—then make sure that you excel in this work of generosity too. I am not saying this as an order, but testing the genuineness of your love against the concern of others. You are well aware of the generosity which our Lord Jesus Christ had, that, although he was rich, he became poor for your sake, so that you should become rich through his poverty.

❦ ❧

Both in this letter and in the letter to the Romans, Paul is much concerned about a collection he is making for God's people at Jerusalem. If 2 Corinthians is indeed composed of several letters, the following chapter may even be an independent letter addressed to the Corinthians in particular, while the present chapter is to the province of Achaia as a whole, of which Corinth was the capital.

When the division of spheres was made between Peter and Paul, with Peter being sent by the church at Jerusalem to the Jews and Paul to the Gentiles, the only request made of Paul was that he should 'remember to help the poor' (Galatians 2:10). The church in Jerusalem seems always to have been in financial difficulty, for many elderly pious people moved there without many resources, resolved to end their days in the Holy City. Then the split (or spat) occurred between Paul and the Jerusalem church, which formed the background of the letter to the Galatians. A collection among the Gentile churches to make a handsome donation to the church at Jerusalem would be seen as a sign of good will and recognition that the faith came to them from Jerusalem. It would be a splendid way to heal the division and hard feeling that had followed. It would also, of course, heal Paul's own damaged reputation among the Jewish Christians. He promised to take the gift to Jerusalem personally if it was significant enough (Romans 15:25).

It is touching to see how anxious Paul is about this collection—and not only because he realized that it was necessary to defend himself against any charge of embezzlement (2 Corinthians 8:20). He both cajoles them to give handsomely and assures them that they should not give beyond their means, as well as complimenting and flattering them as any fundraiser does! The best way is to put aside money in good time, so as to be ready for Paul's messengers when they arrive.

As always, Paul links his practical advice to his theological principles, seeing the generosity of his friends as an echo of Christ's own generosity, who emptied himself for our sake so that we 'should become rich through his poverty' (v. 9).

*Lord, you emptied yourself for our sake. Grant that I too may be generous with my resources in your service.*

# 35

# Chosen in Christ

EPHESIANS 1:3–14

Blessed be God the Father of our Lord Jesus Christ, who has blessed us with all the spiritual blessings of heaven in Christ. Thus he chose us in Christ before the world was made to be holy and faultless before him in love, marking us out for himself beforehand, to be adopted sons, through Jesus Christ. Such was his purpose and good pleasure, to the praise of the glory of his grace, his free gift to us in the Beloved, in whom, through his blood, we gain our freedom, the forgiveness of our sins. Such is the richness of the grace which he has showered on us in all wisdom and insight. He has let us know the mystery of his purpose, according to his good pleasure which he determined beforehand in Christ, for him to act upon when the times had run their course: that he would bring everything together under Christ, as head, everything in the heavens and everything on earth. And it is in him that we have received our heritage, marked out beforehand as we were, under the plan of the One who guides all things as he decides by his own will, chosen to be, for the praise of his glory, the people who would put their hopes in Christ before he came. Now you too, in him, have heard the message of the truth and the gospel of your salvation, and having put your trust in it you have been stamped with the seal of the Holy Spirit of the Promise, who is the pledge of our inheritance, for the freedom of the people whom God has taken for his own, for the praise of his glory.

❧

The letters to the Colossians and to the Ephesians may well not have been written by Paul personally, or even through a secretary. Their style is quite different: they are heavy, overloaded and ponderous, with none of the quick, darting arguments and broken sentences of Paul. Their theology also shows a number of differences from that of Paul. For instance, at the end of this blessing, there is no longer a difficulty about the rejection of Christ by the Jews, but rather the Jews were marked out beforehand to receive the blessing and have now been joined by the Gentiles. Further, Ephesians borrows several phrases word for word from Colossians. So of the two, current opinion is that Colossians was probably by Paul, Ephesians probably not. They may be, however, the first great commentaries on Paul, written by someone thoroughly familiar with his thinking, who wanted to put down what he reckoned Paul would have said in these circumstances.

The blessing at the beginning of Ephesians outlines the plan of God in the history of salvation, 'the mystery of his purpose' (v. 9) from the beginning of the world, now at last revealed in Christ. God had determined to 'bring everything together under Christ, as head' (v. 10: this is all one magnificent word in Greek), to sum up and complete in Christ the whole plan of creation. In 1 Corinthians Paul had taught that Christians together make up the body of Christ, each contributing a special gift. There, the body was considered as the local church in Corinth or in each place. Now the canvas has broadened, and we learn that Christ is the head over the body, which is the whole Church universal. He is to the Church the source of authority, leadership, direction and nourishment. In this letter Christ is contrasted with 'every principality, ruling force, power or sovereignty' (1:21). He is far above them all, in a mysterious phrase, 'the fullness of him who is filled, all in all' (v. 23), having brought creation to its completion by winning our freedom and the forgiveness of our sins through his blood.

*Lord, I am a tiny particle in your immense plan of salvation, and yet each particle has infinite value in your eyes.*

# 36

# Mutual Submission

EPHESIANS 5:21–32

Be subject to one another out of reverence for Christ.
Wives should be subject to their husbands as to the
Lord, since, as Christ is head of the Church and saves
the whole body, so is a husband the head of his wife;
and as the Church is subject to Christ, so should wives
be to their husbands, in everything. Husbands should
love their wives, just as Christ loved the Church and
sacrificed himself for her to make her holy by washing
her in cleansing water with a form of words, so that when
he took the Church to himself she would be glorious,
with no speck or wrinkle or anything like that, but holy
and faultless. In the same way, husbands must love their
wives as they love their own bodies; for a man to love
his wife is for him to love himself. A man never hates his
own body, but he feeds it and looks after it; and that is
the way Christ treats the Church, because we are parts of
his Body. This is why a man leaves his father and mother
and becomes attached to his wife, and the two become
one flesh. This mystery has great significance, but I am
applying it to Christ and the Church.

Towards the end of the letter comes the moral exhortation, a pattern that this letter shares with all Paul's letters. Here Christ's devotion, his generous love for the Church, is movingly compared to the love and devotion of a man for his wife. The striking factor is that Christ's sacrifice for the Church is not adduced as a model that human devotion should attempt to follow, but vice versa: human devotion and sacrifice in marriage are first seen as an image by which Christ's sacrifice may be understood and appreciated. Great as is, and should be, the love of spouses, it is no more than a pale shadow of Christ's love and gift of himself to the Church. Only after that is the relationship of Christ and the Church seen as the perfect example, which the husband's self-sacrifice and the wife's obedience should reflect.

This teaching is often seen in today's world as lopsided: should a wife be subservient to her husband? It is, of course, presented in accordance with the view of a world where the man was dominant. But for a successful marriage both relationships must be reciprocal: the generosity of the husband must be echoed by that of the wife, and the submission of the wife echoed by that of the husband. The passage, after all, starts reciprocally—'be subject to one another', not merely wife to husband. There is then a slight shift: Christ washes his bride, the Church, in the waters of baptism; but the normal bride is prepared to greet her husband not by the husband himself but by her own attendants. The point of comparison is that the bride is presented in all her perfection.

The richness of the teaching on both unions, both the

marital union and the union of Christ and the Church, is intensified by the quotation from Genesis (v. 31). By 'one flesh' is meant not merely bodily, physical union, but that the two become one thinking, living being. In Hebrew thought, a person, one flesh, is an animated body, so that the partners become one single animated body, sharing everything—thoughts, ambitions, desires and jokes.

*Lord, grant to married couples and to your Church the generosity and responsiveness that will enable them to become one flesh.*

# 37

# God's Chosen People

ROMANS 11:13–24

Let me say then to you gentiles that, as far as I am an apostle to the gentiles, I take pride in this work of service; and I want it to be the means of rousing to envy the people who are my own blood-relations and so of saving some of them. Since their rejection meant the reconciliation of the world, do you know what their re-acceptance will mean? Nothing less than life from the dead!

When the first-fruits are made holy, so is the whole batch; and if the root is holy, so are the branches. Now suppose that some branches were broken off, and you are wild olive, grafted among the rest to share with the others the rich sap of the olive tree; then it is not for you to consider yourself superior to the other branches; and if you start feeling proud, think: it is not you that sustain the root, but the root that sustains you. You will say, 'Branches were broken off on purpose for me to be grafted in.' True; they through their unbelief were broken off, and you are established through your faith. So it is not pride that you should have, but fear: if God did not spare the natural branches, he might not spare you either. Remember God's severity as well as his goodness: his severity to those who fell, and his goodness to you as long as you persevere in it; if not, you too will be cut off. And they, if they do not persevere in their unbelief, will be grafted in; for it is within the power of God to graft them back again. After all, if you, cut off from what was by nature a wild olive, could then be grafted unnaturally on to a cultivated olive, how much easier will it be for them, the branches that naturally belong there, to be grafted on to the olive tree which is their own.

❧ ❧

For Paul, the Jew, the failure of so many of his fellow Jews to respond to Christ is an agony. However, the Jews remain for Paul the chosen race, the people of God. Despite being repeatedly punished by the Jews for his Christian option, Paul remains through and through a Jew, proud of his ancestry, thinking like a Jew, basing his faith on the promises to Abraham, using rabbinic methods of argument. 'Is it possible that God abandoned his people?' (11:1). No! It was prophesied that a remnant would return. So Paul is convinced that somehow the Jews will ultimately be saved. He does not fully understand how, and his agonized reflections end with an appeal to the inscrutable wisdom of God: 'We cannot reach to the root of his decisions or his ways' (v. 33).

He sees the rejection of Christ by Israel as a necessary preliminary to the admission of the Gentiles. If Judaism had joyfully welcomed Christ, Christianity might have remained a Jewish phenomenon and it would have been more difficult for the message to spread to the

Gentiles. As it is, Paul invokes the image of the olive tree, a symbol traditionally used for Israel. The image of branches cut off to make room for the ingrafting of new shoots is a dramatic one, but the trouble is that the next stage does not quite work. The image is unsatisfactory from a horticultural point of view. Once dead branches have been cut off, there is no point in grafting them back in: they are dead and will not return to life. In this case we have to suppose that the natural branches somehow retained their life, 'for it is within the power of God to graft them back again'. Perhaps this is why Paul appeals to the inscrutable wisdom of God.

*You too, Lord Jesus, were sprung from the stock of Abraham. Bring your chosen race to acknowledge that you are the Messiah of their hopes.*

# 38

# Christ's Body and Blood

## 1 CORINTHIANS 11:23–29

For the tradition I received from the Lord and also handed on to you is that on the night he was betrayed, the Lord Jesus took some bread, and after he had given thanks, he broke it, and he said, 'This is my body, which is for you; do this in remembrance of me.' And in the same way, with the cup after supper, saying, 'This cup is the new covenant in my blood. Whenever you drink it, do this as a memorial of me.' Whenever you eat this bread, then, and drink this cup, you are proclaiming the Lord's death until he comes. Therefore anyone who eats the bread or drinks the cup of the Lord unworthily is answerable for the body and blood of the Lord.

Everyone is to examine himself and only then eat of the bread or drink from the cup; because a person who eats and drinks without recognizing the body is eating and drinking his own condemnation.

❦

Paul here repeats for us the account of the institution of the Eucharist at the last supper. This is one of two pieces of tradition (the other being 1 Corinthians 15: 3–5) which Paul says he received from the Lord and passed on to his converts. They are obviously pieces that he and they learnt by heart, for the vocabulary and usage are slightly different from Paul's own. There are two slightly different versions of the eucharistic words, one given by Mark and Matthew, the other given by Luke and here by Paul. The former represents the tradition as it was guarded in the Aramaic-speaking tradition, the latter as it was guarded in the Greek-speaking tradition. We are here at the very heart of the gospel tradition, and can see how the most basic facts of all in the Christian tradition were passed on in the primitive Church.

Paul chides the Corinthians for their conduct at the Eucharist, for their behaviour is preventing the Eucharist from being the expression of the body of Christ. The rich bring their own supper and have a good meal, while the poorer members of the community go hungry. This does not show the unity that should prevail in the community. So important is this unity, and the consideration for one another, that it is impossible to tell whether by 'the body of Christ' Paul means the community or the bread that is eaten. The community and the bread are both the body of Christ, with equal reality but in a different way. The selfishness and lack of consideration shown by the Corinthians makes nonsense of this sign, in such a way that the blessing cup is no longer a sharing in the blood of Christ and the loaf no longer a sharing in the body of Christ.

Paul's condemnation then becomes even stronger and more positive. Anyone who eats unworthily of the body of Christ is answerable for the body and blood of the Lord, and is eating and drinking his or her own condemnation. Those who fail in this way share in the guilt of those who led Jesus out to execution.

*Lord, may your Eucharist ever be a true sign of your covenant of love renewed in the Church.*

# 39

# Humility and Exaltation

## PHILIPPIANS 2:1–11

So if in Christ there is anything that will move you, any incentive in love, any fellowship in the Spirit, any warmth or sympathy—I appeal to you, make my joy complete by being of a single mind, one in love, one in heart and one in mind. Nothing is to be done out of jealousy or vanity; instead, out of humility of mind everyone should give preference to others, everyone pursuing not selfish interests but those of others. Make your own the mind of Christ Jesus:

Who, being in the form of God, did not count equality with God something to be grasped. But he emptied himself, taking the form of a slave, becoming as human beings are; and being in every way like a human being, he was humbler yet, even to accepting death, death on a cross. And for this God raised him high, and gave him the name which is above all other names; so that all beings in the heavens, on earth and in the underworld, should bend the knee at the name of Jesus and that every tongue should acknowledge Jesus Christ as Lord, to the glory of God the Father.

Paul seems to be quoting an ancient Christian hymn, for the balance and rhythm of these lines is far too smooth for Paul's own energetic style, and the early Christians were encouraged to compose their own 'hymns and spiritual canticles' and bring them to the assembly for worship. Did Paul hear this hymn and adopt it for his own use?

Christ, the second Adam, is compared to the first Adam. The first Adam wanted to be like God; the second Adam did not think that being in the form of God was something to be exploited. Adam wanted to escape death; Christ accepted death, and death on a cross. Adam was disobedient, Christ obedient unto death. Adam tried to exalt himself; Christ humbled himself.

And the result? Adam was humbled; God raised up Christ. This exaltation of Christ is expressed with staggering force. In a strong assertion of the uniqueness and majesty of God, Isaiah sings, 'All shall bend the knee to me, by me every tongue shall swear, saying, "In the Lord alone are saving justice and strength"' (Isaiah 45:23–24). Now the Pauline hymn takes these phrases and applies them to Christ as deserving the same worship and reverence as the Lord God. Christ is given the name which, in Hebrew, is so sacred that the Jews would not pronounce it, the name which is 'above all other names'. In Greek it was translated *kyrios*, 'the Lord', familiar from the prayer '*Kyrie eleison*, Lord have mercy'. So Christ is put in the place of God by means of this amazing attribution to Jesus of Isaiah's confession of God. It might be thought that such an equation of Jesus to the Lord God would detract from the majesty and glory of God, but the hymn ends by showing that, on the contrary, this confession of Jesus is 'to the glory of God the Father'.

In the Jewish sphere it is meaningless simply to say, 'Jesus is God'. How can a human being be God? Does such an assertion not merely show a failure to understand what God is? In this way, however, Paul shows that Christ deserves the worship and honour due only to God.

*Lord, by your cross and resurrection you have set us free. You are the Saviour of the world.*

# 40

# The Supremacy of Christ

COLOSSIANS 1:15–20

He is the image of the unseen God, the first-born of all creation, for in him were created all things in heaven and on earth: everything visible and everything invisible, thrones, ruling forces, sovereignties, powers—all things were created through him and for him. He exists before all things and in him all things hold together, and he is the Head of the Body, that is, the Church.

He is the Beginning, the first-born from the dead, so that he should be supreme in every way; because God wanted all fullness to be found in him and through him to reconcile all things to him, everything in heaven and everything on earth, by making peace through his death on the cross.

❧

This splendid hymn in praise of Christ falls into two stanzas. The first (vv. 15–18a) centres on Christ's primacy in the creation, the second (vv. 18b–20) on his primacy in the re-creation of the resurrection. With a new depth it completes and develops the Pauline teaching of the position of Christ and the renewal of the world.

The first stanza uses the language of the Wisdom literature of the Old Testament to describe Christ's function in the work of creation: he is the Wisdom of God, through whom God created and continues to create. In the Old Testament, God is so exalted that it is a problem to see how God could stoop to creating the universe. The answer is, 'through his Wisdom'. God's Wisdom is of course divine, yet it is not exactly identical with God, but a personified entity, described as 'a reflection of the eternal light, untarnished mirror of God's active power, and image of his goodness' (Wisdom 7:26). This image is now seen to be Christ, in whom and through whom all things were created, the head of the body, and as such superior to all the powers that were thought to rule the universe. It appears that there must have been some mythology among the Colossians and Ephesians about cosmic powers that ruled the universe, and Paul takes this opportunity to underline Christ's superiority to them.

The second stanza concentrates on the exaltation of the historical Christ through his work on earth, so that 'he should be supreme in every way'. It sums up the themes that we have seen in so many ways in Paul. He is the firstfruits of the resurrection, the model leading the way for all Christians into the resurrection from the dead. He is the fullness of all things (compare Ephesians 1:23). By his obedience on the cross he has reconciled all things to God (compare Romans 5:12–21). The peace he brings not only ends the strife between Jew and Gentile, but brings the cosmos to the ultimate fulfilment of God's plan of creation, restoring the glory that was lost at Adam's fall.

*Lord, grant me to share in the glory of your resurrection, where you are at one with your Father and with all the saints.*

## Appendix

# Reading *40 Days with Paul* through Lent

For those who would like to adopt this book as their reading for Lent, this appendix offers reflections on the (Roman Catholic) lectionary readings for each of the six Sundays leading up to Easter.

The outline below shows how the Sunday readings and reflections (in bold type) fit with the 40 readings in the main body of the book.

Ash Wednesday:      1. The Authority of a Servant
Thursday:               2. The Lighter Side of Paul
Friday:                     3. Strength in Weakness
Saturday:                4. Alive in Christ

*Week One*
**Sunday: The Testing of Jesus in the Desert (see p. 133)**
Monday:                 5. Waiting for Jesus
Tuesday:                 6. Like a Mother
Wednesday:            7. The Day of the Lord
Thursday:               8. Preparing for Judgment
Friday:                     9. Justified by Faith
Saturday:                10. Permeated with Christ

*Week Two*
**Sunday:  The Transfiguration (see p. 135)**

(see p. 135)

Monday:          11. A Sharp Rebuke
Tuesday:         12. Divided Loyalties
Wednesday:       13. Favours of the Spirit
Thursday:        14. The Blessing of Faith
Friday:          15. Sons of God
Saturday:        16. Spiritual Fruit

*Week Three*
**Sunday:  Jesus and the Samaritan (see p. 137)**

Monday:          17. Jesus is Lord
Tuesday:         18. God's Saving Justice
Wednesday:       19. Christ's Obedience
Thursday:        20. Saturated With Christ
Friday:          21. The Inner Struggle
Saturday:        22. The Glory to Come

*Week Four*
**Sunday:  The Cure of the Blind Man (see p. 139)**

Monday:          23. Christ is not Divided
Tuesday:         24. True Wisdom
Wednesday:       25. The Temple of the Spirit
Thursday:        26. The Time is Short
Friday:          27. Respect!
Saturday:        28. Advice to Christian Women

*Week Five*
**Sunday: The Raising of Lazarus (see p. 141)**

Monday:          29. The Body of Christ
Tuesday:         30. The Meaning of Love

| Wednesday: | 31. The Risen Life |
| Thursday: | 32. Saying Yes to God |
| Friday: | 33. Undaunted Suffering |
| Saturday: | 34. Remember the Poor |

*Week Six: Holy Week*

**Sunday: The Sunday of Palms and of the Passion**
**(see p. 142)**

| Monday: | 35. Chosen in Christ |
| Tuesday: | 36. Mutual Submission |
| Spy Wednesday: | 37. God's Chosen People |
| Maundy Thursday: | 38. Christ's Body and Blood |
| Good Friday: | 39. Humility and Exaltation |
| Holy Saturday: | 40. The Supremacy of Christ |

# Sunday: The Testing of Jesus in the Desert

Three elements in the readings set the tone for this Sunday and for the week.

The first reading (Genesis 9:8–15) gives us the story of God's covenant with Noah after the flood. Each year, in each of the three annual cycles of reading, the Church works through the history of salvation, tracing the story of Israel as the nation prepares gradually over the ages for the coming of Christ. The first Sunday looks at the early prehistory of Israel, the second at the covenant with Abraham, the third at the time of Moses, the fourth at the Israelite monarchy and the fifth at the promise of the new covenant. Like all the successive covenants with Israel, God's covenant with Noah is a promise of God's friendship and protection, made with human beings emerging from evil—in this case, the flood by means of which God had cleansed the earth from widespread wickedness. The covenant's 'logo' is the wonderful symbol of the rainbow.

The second reading for today (1 Peter 3:18–22) comments on the flood story, relating it to baptism, by which believers are cleansed by passing through the water. This is a reminder that traditionally Lent is a period in which new Christians are being prepared for baptism on Holy Saturday. This first Sunday is the traditional day for inscription of these new Christians. It can be a reminder to all Christians of preparation for the renewal of baptismal vows on Holy Saturday. So Lent is an opportunity for greater fervour of life and greater intensity of prayer.

The Gospel reading brings us to the testing of Jesus. This year's Gospel (Mark 1:12–15) is brief, containing none of the details of the testing that are familiar from Matthew and Luke. After his baptism, Jesus was led out into the desert. What was his vocation as Servant of the Lord to be? The kingdom of God had at last come near, but what form would it take? Mark shows us Jesus at peace with the wild animals of the desert, a return to the peace of the garden of Eden, and an anticipation of the peace that Isaiah had prophesied the Messiah would bring. The first letters of Paul that we read are looking forward to the final coming of the Messiah.

Week Two

# Sunday: The Transfiguration

In each year of the three-year cycle of readings, this Sunday is dedicated to the transfiguration of Jesus. On this occasion the three chosen disciples are granted an experience of the sublime nature of Jesus on the holy mountain. There he is seen transfigured in glory, accompanied by Moses and Elijah, who had also experienced the awesome glory of the Lord on the holy mountain (Mark 9:2–10). This experience of the divine grandeur of Jesus prepares them for the suffering and humiliation of the Passion, which is to follow. The readings for the week are drawn from the fiery letter to the Galatians. The theme of the letter is that salvation is not to be won by observance of the Jewish Law. It has been won by Christ's fulfilment of the Law and flows to us by adoption to sonship as co-heirs with Christ. This is Paul's first analysis of the saving work of Christ, written in the heat of controversy. His arguments are more fully set out in the letter to the Romans.

The first reading for this Sunday (Genesis 22:1–2, 9–13, 15–18) gives a shortened version of the horrific story of Abraham's obedience, his readiness even to sacrifice his own son. This story serves a twofold purpose. It is the second step of progressing, stage by stage, through the history of salvation in the Old Testament. Furthermore, in their writings the fathers of the Church see Abraham's willingness to sacrifice his son as an image of God's willingness to offer his Son for the redemption of the human race.

The short second reading (Romans 8:31–34) presents Paul's cry of joy in the redeeming love of God. It comes as the climax of his extended consideration, the heart of the letter to the Romans, of the process of Christ's work of salvation, a cry of amazed gratitude to the God 'who will not refuse anything he can give'.

## Week Three

# Sunday: Jesus and the Samaritan

## The first scrutiny of the candidates for baptism

Note: The next three Sundays will focus on the readings for Year One of the three-year cycle of readings. These are the classic readings from the Gospel of John, expressing the mysteries with which the candidates preparing for baptism at Easter are linked. The year 2009 is the second of the cycle, but these Johannine readings may be preferred to the readings set for the second year of the cycle. They have been chosen here as the focus because of their inherent value, their classic quality and their link with the preparation of catechumens. Even if they are not read in the public liturgy, it would be valuable to read at least the great Johannine Gospels of the Sunday in the first cycle.

The Gospel reading for this Sunday is Jesus' dialogue with the Samaritan (John 4:5–42). This contains a good deal of humour. She is cheeky and provocative, and in return Jesus seems almost deliberately to mislead her with his ambiguous sayings, which she understands on one level and Jesus (and the Christian reader) on another. In Judaism the water that gives life is the Law. Here it refers to Jesus' own teaching, as he gradually leads her to wonder at him, to believe in him and eventually to spread his message. This Gospel is ideally suited to the first scrutiny of the catechumens who are preparing for baptism at Easter—for emerging, newly baptised, from the water of life. Do they believe in him and are they willing to accept him and spread his message? The same questions, of course, apply to those who are less new to the faith.

On our journey through the Old Testament in the first readings, we have reached Moses (Exodus 17:3–7). After the grumbling of the people, Moses strikes water from the rock. This is a preparation for the living water, which, after the Samaritan's humorous, cantankerous behaviour, Jesus will give to all who thirst for it. The second reading keeps the concentration on the approaching celebration of the Passion by giving, in a short reading from Romans (5:1–2, 5–8), a wonderfully trinitarian summary of Christian hope: we look forward to God's glory because the Spirit is poured into our hearts through Christ's death for us sinners. Our readings from Romans during the week provide a rich insight into how Paul views the process of salvation.

# Sunday: The Cure of the Blind Man

## The second scrutiny of candidates for baptism

This is another superbly dramatic Johannine reading (John 9), but this time the drama comes not from the humour and ambiguity but from the hostility of the Pharisees and the irony of the situation. The more they attempt to drive a wedge between the cured blind man and Jesus, the more they drive him into Jesus' arms. The more they abuse Jesus, the more loyal to him the man becomes. Midway between them stand the man's parents, who shy away from any commitment for fear of being excluded from the synagogue.

This reading coincides with the second scrutiny of the catechumens. Baptism was often known in the early Church as 'enlightenment'. Where do they and we stand on personal commitment to Jesus? Will they and we be loyal to him or wilt under threat? Our readings from Paul during this week, drawn from his first letter to that difficult community at Corinth, show some of the many and varied ways in which such commitment may be manifested or withheld.

The Sunday Old Testament reading (1 Samuel 16: 1, 6–7, 10–13) has reached the fourth step of salvation history, the anointing of David, first king at Jerusalem and founder of the temple cult. As the anointed leader he prefigures Jesus, and God promises to be a father to his descendants. The second reading (Ephesians 5:8–14) attaches to the Gospel reading, concentrating on light as a metaphor for seeing the truth.

# Sunday: The Raising of Lazarus

## The third and final scrutiny of candidates for baptism

In the Gospel of John, the raising of Lazarus is the immediate prelude to the Passion (John 11:1–45). In a typical Johannine paradox, Jesus' gift of life to Lazarus is the immediate cause of his own death. In the preparation of the candidates for baptism at Easter, the story points to the gift of eternal life through baptism.

The first reading (Ezekiel 37:12–14) indicates the fifth stage of salvation history, the new covenant, when the Lord will raise his people to new life. Ezekiel may have meant primarily the raising of the nation to new life by the return from the Babylonian exile, but his prophecy may also be understood as the personal raising from the tomb to new life. In the progress of revelation, therefore, it prepares for the full understanding of the resurrection in Christ. The second reading (Romans 8:8–11) also focuses on the pledge of the Spirit as the guarantee of resurrection from the dead. Romans 8 is the chapter of the Spirit, looking forward to the eventual renewal in the Spirit of the whole of creation.

# Sunday: The Sunday of Palms and of the Passion

The final Sunday, the Sunday of Holy Week, brings Lent to its climax, for Lent is the preparation for the celebration of the Passion and finally of the resurrection of Christ. Woven into that celebration of the resurrection is the Christian commitment. New Christians, who have been preparing over the 40 days, are received into Christ and into the Church on Holy Saturday at the Easter Vigil, while those who are already Christians are encouraged at the same time to renew their baptismal promises.

The tone for the week is set by the procession of palms, as Jesus is welcomed into Jerusalem as the Messiah, and by the great reading of the Passion (Mark 15:1–39). Two readings precede the Passion. The first is a Song of the Suffering Servant (Isaiah 50:4–7), one of the four Songs of the Suffering Servant in Isaiah that are read in turn on the preliminary days of the week, preparing for the climactic celebrations in the final days. The second reading is the hymn of Philippians 2:6–11, which speaks of Christ emptying himself for our sake, 'even to accepting death, death on a cross'.

The readings given for the weekdays have been chosen to express the tone of the week. For the first two days, the readings express the exalted position of

Christ in the plan of God. For the remaining four days, the Pauline readings are appropriate to the particular mystery celebrated on each day.

# brf

## Resourcing your spiritual journey

**through...**

- Bible reading notes
- Books for Advent & Lent
- Books for Bible study and prayer
- Books to resource those working with
  under 11s in school, church and at home

- Quiet days and retreats
- Training for primary teachers
  and children's leaders
- Godly Play
- Barnabas RE Days

For more information, visit the **brf** website
at **www.brf.org.uk**